Glacier's Historic Hotels & Chalets:
View *with a* Room

by Ray Djuff *and* Chris Morrison

FARCOUNTRY
PRESS

ISBN: 1-56037-170-6

© 2001 Farcountry Press
Text © 2001 Ray Djuff and
Chris Morrison

This book may not not be
reproduced in whole or in part
by any means (with the exception of short quotes for the
purpose of review) without the
permission of the publisher.
For more information on our
books call or write:
Farcountry Press,
P.O. Box 5630,
Helena, Montana 59604,
(406) 443-2842, or
(800) 654-1105

Book catalog appears online at:
www.montanamagazine.com

Printed in Korea

Acknowledgments

View With a Room is the result of a collaborative effort, with many people assisting the authors in ways they might never have realized.

Heartfelt thanks to: Thomas White, curator, and Eileen McCormack, associate curator, James Jerome Hill Reference Library, St. Paul, Minn.; Dallas Lindgren and the workers at the Minnesota Historical Society, St. Paul, Minn.; Deirdre Shaw and her cohorts at the National Park Service archives in West Glacier, Mont.; Lysa Wegman-French, historian, National Park Service, Denver, Colo.; the librarians of the Lethbridge Public Library, Chinook Regional Arch, Lethbridge, Alta.; Cheney Cowles Museum, Spokane, Wash.; Maureen and Mike Mansfield Library, University of Montana, Missoula; Montana State University, Bozeman; Oregon Historical Society, Portland, Ore.; archivists at the Montana Historical Society, Helena, Mont.; and Jennifer King, reference archivist at the American Heritage Center, University of Wyoming, Laramie; and Richard Russack and Burlington Northern Santa Fe Corporation.

Many individuals made contributions to this book, and the authors are grateful to each. Unfortunately, not everyone can be named. A few stand out for special recognition:

Mona Brown, Tony Daffern, Walter Emery, Kevin Franchuk, John Hagen, Kate Hampton, Dan Hays, Howard H. Hays, Jr., William Hays, Rebecca Hill, Bob Jacobs, John Mauff, Karola Miener, Millie Perkins, Richard Schwab, Dale Scott, and Joyce Clarke Turvey.

It was our hope in undertaking this work that we could capture some of the spirit of the "old days" in Glacier Park and remind visitors of what was quickly becoming a rich but forgotten history. The many contributors trusted us with their memories. We hope we've been able to do justice to them.

—Ray Djuff and Chris Morrison

Dedication

To Gina, Monika and Michael
For sharing and encouraging my fascination
with Glacier Park's history.
R.D.

To Jim
For his love and support.
C.M.

3507—BEAR GRASS, GLACIER NAT'L PARK

After trains brought visitors to the park, touring buses—complete with blankets and roll side panels—took them from chalet to chalet. Roe Emery, extreme left, founded Glacier Park Transportation Company in 1914 with the financial backing of Walter C. White of the White Motor Company. Under their agreement, White was the sole supplier of buses to the concession. Above is a TEB model White outside Glacier Park Hotel in 1916. The White buses were built using a long (140-inch) wheelbase, ¾-ton truck chassis with 45-hp GEC engines. Drivers earned the nickname "gear-jammers" from the trouble they had double-clutching to shift the four-speed transmissions.

Foreword

Dear Reader,

I hope you find as much enjoyment in this book as I have. The construction of these hotels was an epic surely worthy of Darryl F. Zanuck. This work clearly portrays a history of the construction of the various lodges and also brings forth many of the conflicts that had to be resolved in their construction and operation. Mrs. Morrison and Mr. Djuff have spent many painstaking hours sifting through construction details and also interpreting the human side of the venture.

Their story presents a very human side in that many conflicts beginning with the earliest construction and still existing today had to be dealt with. It encompasses man coping with nature, the railroad and concessioners coping with the National Park Service, the park service coping with the railroad, and all of the above coping with the visitor, whose tastes, expectations and capacities have changed dramatically since 1910.

If you think about it, the railroad started out with the expectation that the park was its destination resort. The National Park Service, on the other hand, was more attuned to its role in presenting and maintaining a hiker's park and interpreting and preserving the natural and cultural environment. Compounding the difficulties presented by these divergent views was the fact that the railroad's budget and the park service's were never in alignment and were determined entirely by different parties with different motivations.

The authors give a fascinating glimpse of the railroad's early enthusiasm waning over the years as more and more Americans went out and bought their own iron horse from Henry Ford rather than continuing to use the railroads.

I would like to thank the authors for an intriguing read and a job well done.

Louis F. Hill
Grandson of Louis W. Hill, Sr.
St. Paul, MN
November 2000

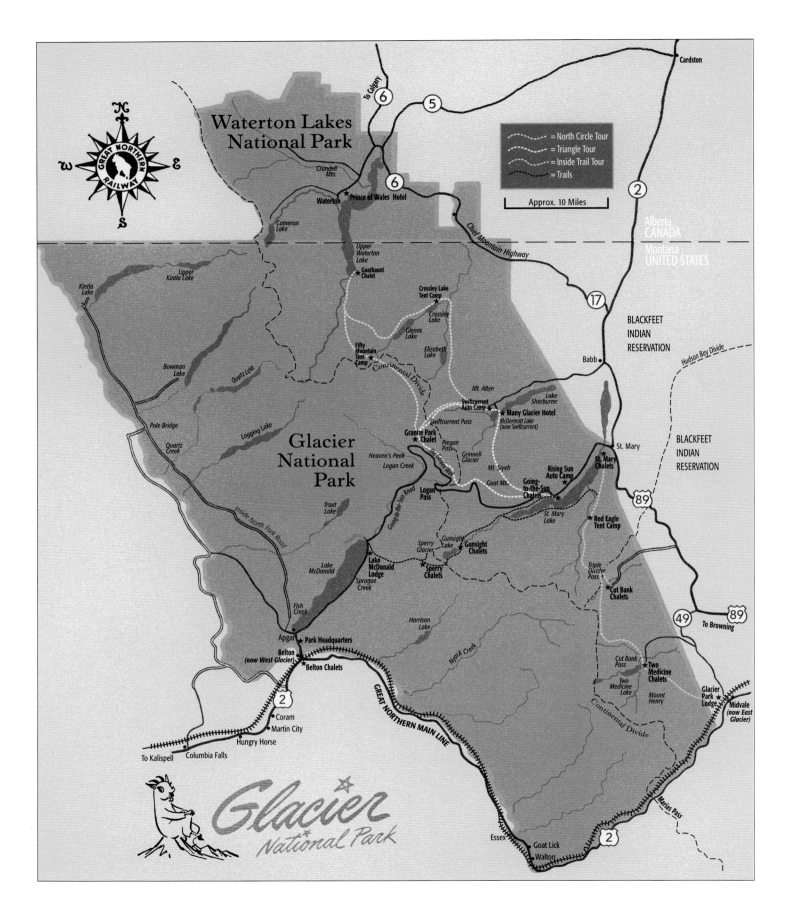

Contents

The call of the Mountains

Vacations in
Glacier National Park

— Chapter One —

The Call of the Mountains

No matter where you travel in and around Glacier National Park, Montana, the legacy of the Great Northern Railway is to be found. From trails and roads constructed with its money to train stations it built and tour boats it commissioned, at every turn is some reminder of the railway whose name ceased to exist in 1970. For most of the 1.5 million visitors who annually tour the park's glacier-carved, U-shaped valleys, three grand, rustic lodges provide the most obvious evidence of this now-defunct railroad's presence: Glacier Park Lodge in the east, Many Glacier Hotel in the center, and Lake McDonald Lodge in the west. Only with some probing do tourists learn that these three survive from what were a dozen hotel and chalet complexes in this north-west corner of Montana, where the Rockies cross into Alberta. St. Paul, Minnesota-based Great Northern operated them for five decades before it left the concession business in 1960.

The man responsible for them was Louis Warren Hill, christened the "godfather of Glacier" for his pivotal work in developing tourism here. Louis Hill, always referred to as "Louie Hill," was the son of James Jerome Hill, founder of Great Northern Railway. "Empire Builder" J.J. Hill justly earned his nickname. He stands alone in American history as the man who built a railway, from Chicago to Seattle, mostly with private capital and earned revenues rather than relying on government land grants, subsidies or loan guarantees.

Born in May 1872, Louis was one of J.J. Hill's ten children, three of whom were sons. He followed his father into the railroad business, start-ing in 1893 and working his way through eighteen different positions. In 1907 the dedicated Louis was named president of the Great Northern, then one of the mightiest railways in the United States. Its empire includ-ed control of the Northern Pacific, and the Chicago, Burlington and Quincy railroads.

Louis Hill, became interested in Glacier's tourist potential in the early 1900s. For a decade, people like Dr. Lyman Sperry and George Bird

Louis Warren Hill, Sr.

Above: "Empire Builder" James Jerome Hill.

Below: This Fred Kiser photo from 1910 shows passengers enjoying the trip through Marias Pass on a platform on the back car of the Oriental Limited. Later, special platform cars were constructed so passengers could take the fifty-seven-mile trip in the open, weather permitting. The platform cars were replaced by observation cars and, later still, dome cars.

Grinnell had been advocating the Glacier region be made a nature preserve. As owner and editor of the popular *Forest and Stream*, Grinnell had a particularly powerful weekly platform from which to make known his opinions. Grinnell first visited Glacier in 1885. He returned repeatedly to the "walled in lakes," each visit increasing his conviction that this special place deserved recognition and protection. It was he who coined the phrase "The Crown of the Continent" to describe Glacier in an article published in the September 1900 issue of *Century* magazine. Over time, lobbying by Grinnell, Sperry and others made inroads, and by 1907 a bill before Congress proposed the national park. It was the first of three attempts to get the legislation passed.

From the beginning, Louis Hill was on Grinnell's side. He appreciated Glacier's spectacular beauty, and he also knew the value of a national park linked to Great Northern's mainline, which ran along the proposed border over Marias Pass. In wanting to tie the railroad to Glacier, Hill was following a trend that began with Northern Pacific and Yellowstone National Park. Yellowstone, and later Glacier, appealed to the curiosity of the Industrial Age's burgeoning middle and upper middle classes about the wonders of nature and the western frontier. Inspired by the pantheist-conservationist movements, the exhortations of outdoor activists John Muir and Teddy Roosevelt, and by what they'd seen in publications such as *National Geographic*, *Sunset*, and *Wonderland*, these nouveau riche were ready to head for the great outdoors. National parks and monuments were relatively novel in 1910, numbering fewer than a dozen, and most had been created only recently, between 1890 and 1908. This was the Gilded Age and those who could afford to seek solace in the wilderness wanted an outdoor experience with all the comforts of home.

Northern Pacific's "adoption" of Yellowstone, and its early monopoly on transportation—making the park in effect the railway's private tourist destination— paid off handsomely,

G. N. RY. HOTELS GLACIER PARK MONT.

and was soon mimicked by other rail lines. William Van Horne, the portly, cigar-puffing president of the Canadian Pacific, probably put the railways' philosophy best: "Since we can't export the scenery, we'll have to import the tourists." Hill had the same notion, which he put it in more economic terms: "The railroads are greatly interested in the passenger traffic to the parks. Every passenger that goes to the national parks, wherever he may be, represents practically a net earning."

Hill had plenty of reason to study the techniques of the Northern Pacific—it was, after all, part of the family business. J.J. Hill and J.P. Morgan were partners in the Northern Pacific, having taken control in November 1900. The Great Northern and Northern Pacific had their headquarters in the same building on Jackson Street in St. Paul. A national park in Glacier would provide the Great Northern with a showpiece to equal Canadian Pacific's Banff and Northern Pacific's Yellowstone. The rival railway lines ran, respectively, parallel to the north and the south of the Great Northern. So when it looked like a bill to create Glacier Park was about to stumble in Congress for a third time, Hill sent telegrams to two committee members urging them to push through the legislation. His intervention helped, and on May 11, 1910, President William Howard Taft signed the bill creating Glacier National Park.

From 1910 to 1913, Louis Hill commissioned construction of nine chalet groups in and around Glacier, as well as his showpiece Glacier Park Hotel at Midvale (now East Glacier Park). Work was begun on chalets at St. Mary, Sun Point, Sperry, Granite Park, Cut Bank, Gunsight Lake, Two Medicine, McDermott (now Swiftcurrent) Lake, and Belton (now West Glacier).

Construction is nearly complete on the lobby section of Glacier Park Hotel in this late spring 1913 photograph. At left is the chalet, called Camp 1, which had served guests for the 1912 season. A pipe running up the slope provided a temporary water supply from Midvale Creek. Before the hotel opened in June, the spur line from the main railroad track and most of the temporary buildings were removed.

The bright red buses of the Glacier Park Transportation Company await the Oriental Limited, which has just pulled up at Glacier Park Station. Many guests preferred to walk to the hotel, passing under the arch built in 1913 with surplus logs from the hotel's construction. After the archway was partly knocked down in a 1920 windstorm, it was removed. Railway officials discussed getting "tornado" insurance but decided the cost of premiums was too great.

With the exception of the area around Lake McDonald, which had seen tourism development prior to the creation of the park, Great Northern controlled just about everything in Glacier. No concessions operated east of the Continental Divide without its input. While the Department of the Interior, and later the National Park Service, issued permits for tour boat, saddle horse, and shuttle bus businesses, the railway signed private agreements allowing the concessions to operate between its hotels and chalets. These deals involved a cut of the profits.

Hill treated the developments in Glacier as a personal project. "The work is so important, I loathe to entrust the development to anybody but myself," he said. It's been speculated that Hill's absorption in Glacier was why he stepped down in 1912 as president of the Great Northern to become chairman of the board, succeeding his father. Louis Hill certainly seemed as if he were ready to move to the park and run the show.

Pleased over Great Northern's interest in Glacier, the Department of the Interior tried to be accommodating, offering twenty-year leases and selling the railway permits to cut trees "for the improvement of the park."

Hill selected most of the hotel and chalet sites personally. He also chose the architectural style for the buildings—the Swiss chalet, in its various manifestations. Hill had a personal fascination with Swiss chalets; his summer home in North Oaks, outside St. Paul, was done in that style. The choice for Glacier was not accidental. Hill wanted to portray the park as "America's Switzerland" to appeal to well-heeled Eastern tourists who might otherwise vacation in Europe. Swiss chalet style had been established as a vernacular form of American architecture in the Adirondacks, where wealthy New Yorkers vacationed in post–Civil War summers. Railways adopted and adapted the style to lodges they built, starting with Old Faithful Inn in Yellowstone, creating what is now called "parkitecture." There was a practical side to Hill's choice: the Swiss design with its large roof overhangs is well suited to carry heavy snow loads found in the Rockies, resist winds, and offer shelter from the elements.

To accommodate visitors while Glacier Park Lodge and the chalets were under construction, Hill arranged with Midvale businessman William J. Hilligoss to establish a series of "tent camps" (some of the tents being wooden shacks). They opened in 1911, most located near chalet colony construction sites.

It quickly became clear that poor roads and lack of trails would be a major obstacle to developing tourism in Glacier. There were at the time only two serviceable trails in the park—Sperry/Gunsight/St. Mary Lake, and Swiftcurrent Pass/Granite Park/Lake McDonald—and no roads worthy of the name. With a budget of a mere $15,000 for 1911, there was little that park superintendent William Logan could do to start on all that needed to be done. To ensure immediate access for tourists, as well as for its construction crews and contractors hauling supplies, the Great Northern put up the money to rebuild the road from Midvale to Many Glacier. The cost was $90,900—six times the total park budget for the year.

Railway officials would later boast that in the first ten years of Glacier Park's existence, Great Northern spent $10 for every $1 allocated by Washington. That figure is disputed. Historian James Sheire says that by 1917 the government had spent $634,000 compared to approximately $1.5 million by the railway. Whatever the ratio, Great Northern's investment was substantial enough that its officials took more than a passing interest in how Glacier Park was being run, and whether the railway benefited.

Hill was particularly outspoken,

*Rain-soaked roads played havoc with bus schedules, so teams of horses were kept ready at known mudholes. Even when dry, the roads were a problem. Flat tires were epidemic, in part because the buses were overloaded; eventually the passenger count was reduced to nine from eleven. **Below:** Because the buses' signboards repeatedly fractured, the signs were abandoned by 1917.*

Above: *Maj. William Logan was in the Indian Service before being appointed Glacier's first superintendent in 1910. A one-time scout with Custer, he had been through the region in 1883 as a packer for Prof. Raphael Pumpelly's expedition. Logan's term was short; he died in February 1912.*

Below: *Louis Hill, seated by the driver, soon decided stagecoaches would not do in Glacier. During 1913 and 1914, stagecoaches worked side by side with tour cars and buses; after a stagecoach ran off the road when its horses were spooked by a motor vehicle, coaches were abandoned.*

rapping Logan, for instance, for spending his entire 1911 appropriation on residences for park staff and roads, both on the west side of Glacier, while investing nothing east of the Continental Divide where Great Northern had its operations. When Logan died in February 1912 and was temporarily replaced by Robert Chapman, Hill was equally critical. "Mr. Chapman has not done anything as yet in the park that has been of any particular value," Hill wrote Chapman's supervisor. It was no help that the 1912 appropriation for Glacier, $69,200, did not arrive until August 24, more than halfway through the season. And while boosted from the previous year, it was woefully inadequate, considering the estimate for needed road and trail work came to $232,150.

Railway officials were not above blatant attempts to influence park administration, even going so far as trying to have a railway employee appointed as Logan's replacement. When the Secretary of the Interior balked, Hill switched his backing to James L. Galen, brother of Montana Attorney General Albert Galen. The railway's bald-faced attempt at influence peddling quickly came to the attention of President Taft, who was asked to decide the matter.

"There is a lot of pressure to appoint Galen," Secretary of the Interior Walter Fisher noted. Despite concerns about how it might be perceived as catering to the railway, Galen was appointed superintendent on December 1, 1912. Even so, Hill was not entirely satisfied. Over the next five years he wrote an unrelenting stream of mail telegrams criticizing Galen and all manner of park and Department of Interior operations.

Hill's unflagging attention to matters affecting Glacier park protected not only the railway's investment, but also that of other entrepreneurs he persuaded to participate in the venture. "We do not wish to go into the hotel business," Hill told a conference of national park concessioners in 1911. "We wish to get out of it and confine ourselves strictly to the business of getting peo-

ple there just as soon as we can. But it is difficult to get capital interested in this kind of pioneer work. With co-operation and assistance of the government, we hope within two or three years to get financial people interested in the park and then we can get out and attend to railroading."

The first important investors Hill brought on board were William and James Brewster. The Brewster brothers were renowned outfitters in Banff, and Hill hoped to use their experience in Glacier. He enticed them to set up a saddle horse and stagecoach concession in 1912 to operate between the teepee/tent camps, some of which the railway took over from Hilligoss. Where tour boats were needed, Hill commissioned boat-builder Captain William Swanson to construct the necessary vessels and run them under contract for the railway. Later, Swanson set up his own tour boat concession.

The fruition of Hill's efforts in Glacier came in 1913 with the opening of the chalet colonies and Glacier Park Lodge for their first summer season.

The railway's advertising and publicity department kicked into overdrive. Glacier is a place where the air "blows you alive with vigor" and "your eyes view a region of beauty at your feet, your ears hear the music of the primitive world and heed the silences of great places," the railway boasted in an advertisement in *National Geographic*. "You can enjoy all this wonder from 'quaint little hotel colonies' or the 'novel and interesting'" Glacier Park Hotel where "every room is electrically lighted and heated. Every modern feature, including shower baths and plunge pool, has been installed. The cuisine is worthy of the finest eastern establishment. The rates—American plan $2 to $5 a day."

Some 12,000 people ventured to Glacier that summer, a 100-percent jump in visitation from the previous year. The overwhelming majority arrived aboard a Great Northern train. Public reaction was flatteringly

Exhilarating MOUNTAIN AIR

Take a deep breath—and another. Have you ever breathed air as it came down from mountain tops? Air that had whipped over glaciers, crystal lakes, flashing streams, and evergreen forests? With air of such delicious freshness as to make you tingle from head to toe is mingled the resinous incense of dried pine needles. Imagine yourself transported and set down in a land of fabulous mountains where slopes and jagged peaks are splashed and banded by great masses of color—tawny golds, greens, wine reds and purples. Great evergreen forests mantle the slopes or cling to sheer rock walls up to timberline. Here, glacial lakes in peacock blues and emerald greens stud the valley or are bound up in rocky cirques like jewels in a setting. Streams of crystal clear waters rush and tumble through the valleys or fling themselves with reckless abandon from mountain sides in great cascades. You feel exhilarated—alive—and a great sense of peace and well being comes upon you. "Man oh man", what this does to your appetite and how you sleep at night! There is nothing like it. This year make your vacation the most memorable one you ever enjoyed. You are extended a hearty western welcome to Glacier National Park where

SEEING
EATING
SLEEPING
are such genuine pleasures

BELOW. *Foaming, dashing mountain streams provide Nature's crescendo.*
RIGHT. *You will see Trick Falls near Two Medicine Chalets on motor-coach tours.*

The railway distributed its promotional materials widely, intending to show in words and photos the "mountain experience" of Glacier: romping, eating and sleeping amid clear skies and incredible panoramas. The above is from a 1950s brochure.

Among trail guides' duties was making coffee for riders at rest stops, such as this one near Hanging Glacier. Each boxed lunch carried on day trips contained an individual coffee packet for guides to collect, and a collapsible coffee cup. An inscription on later lunch boxes read: "Here's to a happy, healthy lark/Upon the trails of GLACIER Park."

positive and Hill, flush with renewed enthusiasm, was ready to expand his tourist mecca. He drove to Waterton Lakes National Park, across the Montana-Alberta border in Canada, to pick a site for what would become the Prince of Wales Hotel. He also approved addition of a bedroom annex to Glacier Park Hotel. In the summer of 1914, he selected the spot for Many Glacier Hotel.

The true genius of the accommodations was in Hill's site selection. Each location had a dramatically different scenic backdrop. Hill ensured the buildings were placed so guests could enjoy a view from every room. The use of the same rustic Swiss style for all the chalets ensured guests never lost the feeling of being somewhere special and far away. It created a sense of place in a region of immense proportions.

The hotels and chalets were positioned a comfortable day's ride apart for tourists taking saddle horse vacations. For that is how Hill envisioned visitors seeing Glacier—on horseback. Going-to-the-Sun Highway (now Road) across the Continental Divide was more than two decades away when the chalets opened in 1913. Saddle horse trips were the easiest method to see the park's interior, and its diverse terrain and environments. Later, permanent tent camps at Fifty Mountain, Red Eagle Lake, Goat Haunt, and Crossley (now Cosley) Lake would supplement the chalets.

The linchpin to the success of this hotel and chalet system was accessibility. Tourists had to reach and depart their destinations on time to keep reservations, prevent double booking, and make transportation connections. Unfortunately, the Brewsters couldn't manage it. After complaints about late stagecoaches and mix-ups with saddle horse tours in 1912, Hill refused to offer the Brewsters a long contract. The May 1913 deal for saddle horse and stage service was for just a year. Bill Brewster supplemented his services with motor cars as a way to get passengers through muddy roads when rain sidelined his three stagecoaches. Problems persisted, however. As a result, Hill offered the Brewsters another one-year contract for 1914, adding a proviso that Great

Northern maintained the right to offer automobile and auto-bus services in the park. What the Brewsters didn't know was that Hill had been having secret discussions with Walter White of the White Motor Company in Cleveland about testing buses on Glacier's roads. After a successful bus trial in 1914, the Brewsters lost the concession to the Glacier Park Transportation Company, partly owned and subsidized by White and operated by Roe Emery.

Hill would brook nothing less than excellence. Within two years, the Brewsters, and others, were squeezed out of the saddle horse concession when Wilbur N. Noffsinger, a Kalispell, Montana, lawyer, consolidated and began to operate these services as the Park Saddle Horse Company, which had exclusive reign in Glacier for three decades.

But Great Northern faced its own operational difficulties, most particularly after Glacier Park developments grew beyond Hill's personal control. It became clear that a central organization was needed and, in May 1914, the railway established Glacier Park Hotel Company, with its own managers and staff. Howard Noble eventually became president and general manager, watched over by Hill as chairman of its board. Other key railway officials filled the rest of the board.

Noble ran the hotel company with a small group of full-time employees, most of whom served double duty. During the off-season they handled reservations, promotion, advertising, and hiring. Each summer, when the headquarters moved from Great Northern's twelve-story headquarters building in St. Paul to the basement of Glacier Park Hotel, the duties shifted to the day-to-day operations.

Since the hotels and chalets operate only during the summer, June 15 to September 15, staffing was problematic. The hotel company sought teachers and retired professionals to fill key departmental positions at each site. The remainder of the staff were college-age students. Initially, the hotel company looked no farther than around St. Paul for employees. The reason was simple: it allowed interviews with potential workers. The hotel company favored the children of railway employees, knowing the level of loyalty and trust would be higher since any indiscretion would reflect on the parent. Having a friend whose parent worked for the Great Northern could also garner the necessary recommendation for a summer job. But, as word of jobs spread through the college grapevine, applications began to pour in from across the country.

Students would go to great lengths to work in the park. Despite a preference for hiring those over twenty-one, the railway occasionally hired

Above: William and James Brewster, first and second from left in a family grouping here, were enticed by Louis Hill to set up saddle horse and stagecoach services between the Great Northern's hotels and chalets in Glacier. They were unable to transfer their success in Banff National Park, Alberta, to Glacier; by 1915 they were out of the concession business in the American park.

Below: Brochures summarized trail rides, routes and prices.

SADDLE HORSE TRIPS
in GLACIER
NATIONAL
PARK

Great Northern Railway

17

The "bubble queens" ruled the laundry. This 1928 crew did not only bedding, towels and dining room linens for Glacier Park Hotel, but also laundry from Two Medicine and Cut Bank chalets. A boiler room produced hot water and steam to drive pulleys that ran the equipment. A series of large, heated rollers called "the mangler" pressed laundry, with two or more women feeding in sheets and pillow cases on one side and a group folding on the other.

Joan Shipley

younger people. Eighteen-year-old Joan Shipley (nee Fritz) used bravado with interviewer Ralph Erickson to land work for herself and friend Emily Van Dusen.

"His first question was: How old are you," Shipley recalled. "I said 18. He folded my application and said: 'Well, you know you have to be 21.'

"I quickly retorted with: 'But Mr. Erickson, I'm far more qualified than some of the girls who are already accepted, and who are not 21. I'm not going to lie about my age. The Finley girl and her friend are going because they have pull. Mr. Finley is vice-president of the Great Northern. They have no waitress experience at all. I've worked my way through high school as a waitress. I have two years' experience.... They're going for a joyride. I have to earn money for college and I need this job because I have to work my way through.'

"'Young lady, can you carry a tray with 12 dinners on it, balanced on your shoulder with one hand while you pass through a swinging door from the kitchen to the dining room?' Erickson asked.

"I said: 'No, but I can learn!'

"'You're in!,' he said."

A job at the hotels and chalets in Glacier may have been prized, but was also demanding. The employee handbook set out the high standard expected: "The ideal of this organization is…to please and satisfy our guests, to perform every act of service quickly, quietly, cheerfully, and courteously and to let no guest depart feeling that everything and more was not done to make his visit with us something to look back upon with pleasure." Managers were gruff at the beginning of the season in an effort to get employees in line quickly. There was little tolerance for anyone who wouldn't follow the rules. Being dismissed could pose a serious problem since the railway paid for the trip from St. Paul to the park, but refused return fare if an employee failed to fulfill his contract to the specified termination date. The hotel company was finicky about this, since it needed certain staffing levels throughout the summer, with enough people on hand for opening and closing.

The railway paid notoriously low wages to summer employees, but with a plan. First-year workers did the grunt jobs as busboys, maids and launderers, with the promise next season of a chance for the prized positions of waitress or bellhop, where the potential for huge tips offset poor pay. As a shoeshine boy at Many Glacier Hotel in 1947, Richard Rohleder of St. Paul earned $100 a month, and "saved about $375 in tips. The next year I was a bellman, made $30 a month, paid $75 for my uniform, $5 for the medical and at the end of the summer proudly showed my parents thirteen $100 bills I'd made in tips." And students did return, as much for the camaraderie that developed among the "coolie labor" as for an opportunity to spend a summer in the mountains.

Even after the setup of Glacier Park Hotel Company, Louis Hill was never far removed from day-to-day affairs. Hotel company executives made a point of ensuring he received copies of all important memos, and that he was consulted on matters big and small. But sometimes staff misjudged Hill's interests. He once made a passing comment about the tea served at Glacier Park Hotel, asking if it was possible to get orange pekoe. Howard Noble sent for samples from California then passed them on for Hill's opinion. Hill's assistant "called Mr. Noble and told him Mr. Hill doesn't want to select the tea; he may get whatever he wants."

The result of Hill's attention to detail, and insistence the hotel company be run at a very high standard, was a large volume of repeat business

The Great Northern distributed "aeroplane" maps to encourage people to take its trains to Glacier National Park. Airline service to the park was decades away, but the maps gave potential rail travelers a bird's eye view of geographical features and hotel and chalet locations. Charles Lindbergh's flight over Glacier in late 1927, on a tour following his Atlantic crossing, added cachet to the aeroplane maps.

19

Above: *Photographer Tomer J. Hileman of Kalispell, far right, took publicity shots of Glacier for the Great Northern, early 1920s to late 1930s. A graduate of the Effingham (Illinois) School of Photography, he specialized in scenics, seldom using people in pictures because changing clothing styles dated the images. Hileman was fearless, climbing to any mountain location, large-format camera and equipment in tow, to get the right shot.*

Below: *Louis Hill, standing fourth from left, explored much of the Glacier area before it received national park status in 1910, sometimes accompanied by members of the Blackfeet tribe. Chief Two Guns White Calf, front row right, became Hill's friend and helped with park publicity. Hill commissioned Blackfeet chiefs to record tribal history in pictographs displayed in the lobbies of hotels and one chalet in the park.*

and excellent word-of-mouth promotion. With the exception of a brief interlude, 1918-1919 when the railways were under federal management during World War I, rail arrivals at Glacier Park climbed steadily though slowly throughout the 1910s and into the 1920s. By 1929, 70,000 people a year were visiting, with 10,000 arriving by train. The rest came by private automobile. This was the golden era for railway travel in the twentieth century.

With ever-greater numbers of tourists arriving in Glacier, Hill had little trouble persuading other Great Northern board members to continue expanding the railway's developments. After Many Glacier Hotel opened in 1915, an eighty-room annex and swimming pool were approved at the site; the tent camps at Sperry and Granite Park were replaced by permanent structures; and more bedrooms were added to Going-to-the-Sun Chalets. In 1925, Hill finally got around to his decade-old proposal for a hotel in Waterton. Construction on the ninety-room Prince of Wales Hotel started in 1926 and was finished in 1927.

The railway's investment in the parks now exceeded $2.3 million, and Hill was still not done. He authorized negotiations to buy the Lewis (Glacier) Hotel on Lake McDonald. By 1930, the railway owned it, newly renamed Lake McDonald Hotel, well in time to capitalize on the opening of Going-to-the-Sun Highway three years later.

The Great Northern promoted the park with a steady stream of advertising and publicity brochures. Four years after the park was created the railway was spending upwards of $300,000 annually to promote travel there. The money paid for renowned magazine and novel writer Mary Roberts Rinehart to submit copy for brochures. Artists John Fery of Chicago and Adolph Heinz were commissioned to produce landscapes that were reproduced in color in brochures to supplement the black and white photography of Fred Kiser, R.E. Marble and, later, Tomer Hileman. On radio, the railway sponsored coast-to-coast broadcasts of *Empire Builders* on NBC to promote the park and help publicize Great Northern's train of the same name.

William P. Kenney, vice-president of the railway, said to Hill: "The park has been so thoroughly advertised through so many mediums that it has been almost impossible for people to keep from knowing about the park through some source or another."

The railway's advertising played on the romance of the western frontier, using Native American imagery as its major theme. The focus was on the Blackfeet whose reservation borders the park, and from which part of Glacier was created. They were renamed "the Glacier Park Indians" by the railway. The Great Northern's advertising department subsidized James Willard Schultz, selling copies of his *Blackfeet Tales of Glacier National Park*. Members of the Blackfeet tribe also made it onto the silver screen, with the Great Northern's help, having roles in the Lyman Howe travelogue *A Day in the Life of a Glacier Park Indian* (1915) and Marshall Neilan's film *Bob Hampton of Placer* (1920).

Louis Hill was personally involved with the company's promotional efforts. He accompanied a contingent of Blackfeet to the Panama-Pacific Exposition in San Francisco in 1915. He invited or commissioned artists including Julius Seyler, W. Langdon Kihn, Kathryn Leighton, and Winold Reiss to paint the Blackfeet. Hill ensured that members the Chicago Geographical Society, the Seattle Mountaineers, and the Sierra Club of California received sponsored (often all-expense-paid) trips to Glacier. Then their travelogues were printed by the railway and distributed.

Hill maintained his grip on the railway's Glacier Park operations until 1929, when he stepped down as chairman of the board of Great Northern. It would have appeared appropriate timing: The economy was booming; tourism to Glacier was at an all-time high; and Great Northern had just introduced the *Empire Builder*, named in tribute to J.J. Hill, as its first-class train. But, within months of Louis Hill's departure, America was in the midst of

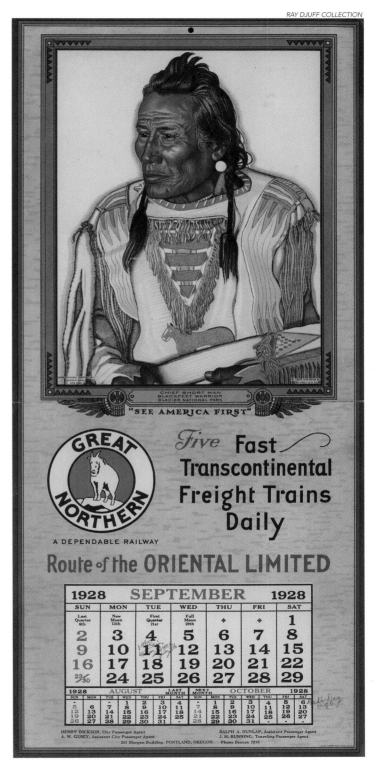

Nineteen-twenty-eight was the first year Great Northern calendars featured Winold Reiss paintings.

21

Glacier Park Station was a bee-hive of activity twice a day, with the arrivals of the Oriental Limited *(later, the* Empire Builder*). For many years train tickets were good for stopovers in Glacier—from overnight to a month. Travelers could get off at the depot in the morning, have lunch at Going-to-the-Sun or Two Medicine chalets, stay the night at one of the hotels and be back on the train the following morning—a mini-vacation. Tourists to Glacier Park continued to arrive by rail until the 1970s, when bus trips and airplane flights superseded rail as preferred modes of long-distance travel.*

the worst economic depression of the century. Passenger traffic to Glacier nose-dived to its lowest level since the park was created. The Great Northern tried to counter loss of traffic by cutting fares. It made little impact. Rail tours to Glacier were so low that in 1933 the hotel company didn't bother opening Cut Bank or St. Mary chalets, or the Prince of Wales Hotel.

Without passenger business, hotel operation became an increasing financial burden. Kenney, by then president of the Great Northern, groused: "We must rid ourselves of all these parasites as quickly as possible." A few years before, when the railroad was prosperous, it did not mind writing off the annual deficits of the Glacier Park Hotel Company. With the onset of the Depression, the directors scanned costs very closely.

The chalet and hotel closures forced Great Northern officials to tackle an issue that they had long ago noted but failed to address: automobile tourism. Automobiles came into their own in the 1920s as reliability increased, and newly improved roads brought the West within reach of residents in populous Eastern and Midwestern states. Where one in every two tourists to Glacier arrived by car in 1920, the ratio was nine auto-travelers to every one rail arrival by 1930. The opening of Roosevelt Highway, between Midvale and Belton in 1930, and Going-to-the-Sun Highway in 1933 ended Great Northern's monopoly on travel in and around Glacier Park. And motels, cabin camps, and other facilities operated by private entrepreneurs, all outside park boundaries, competed for customers.

The opening of Rising Sun (originally called East Glacier) Auto Cabins and restaurant/camp store in 1940 came after a long feud between the Great Northern and National Park Service officials over the hotel concession license and how far the railway had to go to serve tourists not on its organized trips. It was more than fifteen years after travel by private vehicles really took off in Glacier that the railway deigned to build facilities to serve the needs of "auto-tourists."

Strongly encouraged by the National Park Service, the Glacier Park Hotel Company opened an "auto-cabin camp" at Swiftcurrent in 1934, followed by another at Roes Creek (now called Rose Creek or Rising Sun) in 1941. The success of these early motels posed a problem for Great Northern officials. Cheap to build and rent ($2.50 a day compared to $6.50 to $14 for a hotel or chalet room), they were popular with tourists but drew away traffic from the hotels. These new auto-tourists were also less likely to use the Park Saddle Horse Company, since they could see much of the park from their cars. Fewer long saddle horse trips meant lower guest counts at Great Northern's chalets. It was a vicious circle, made more ironic by the work of the Civilian Conservation Corps, which had put Glacier's trails in the best condition they'd ever been.

The fact is the luster of owning hotels and chalets in Glacier wore off for Great Northern executives during the 1930s. Once a symbol of Louis Hill's personal prowess and of Great Northern's corporate prestige, they became only financial burdens. Outwardly, railway officials never let on how they felt, but it was the beginning of the end for Great Northern's involvement in Glacier Park.

After World War II, the Great Northern did not re-open three of its chalet complexes: Going-to-the-Sun, St. Mary, and Cut Bank. The Park Saddle Horse Company had folded during the war, so the chalets were no longer needed. Dilapidated by exposure to Glacier's harsh elements, neglect during the Depression, and disuse, the three complexes were torn down.

Three other chalets, Belton, Sperry, and Granite Park, were sold, leav-

CHICAGO, TWIN CITIES AND PACIFIC NORTHWEST—Continued.

Westbound—Read Down									Eastbound—Read Up					
Motor	Motor	Oriental Limited	Empire Builder	Miles	**TABLE 6** Mountain Time		Altitudes	Miles	Empire Builder	Oriental Limited		Motor	Motor	
231 Ex Sun	**229** Daily	**41** Daily	**3** Daily	**1** Daily					**2** Daily	**4** Daily	**42** Daily	**230** Ex Sun	**232** Ex Sun	
	3 55				850	Lv Savoy .... Ar	2328	915					10 10	f10 00
	f 4 05				856	" Matador (Little Rocky Lv	2332	909					9 50	f 9 40
						Mts. 40 miles south)								
	4 15		2 02		862	" Harlem (Ft. Belknap Ind. Agcy.) "	2371	903			3 47		9 50	f 9 40
	f 4 25				868	" Fort Belknap (Gros Ventres "	2373	897						
						Indians, Snake Butte)							9 30	
	4 35				874	" Zurich .... "	2384	891					9 20	f 9 20
	f 4 40				877	" North Fork .... "	2394	888					f 9 10	
	4 55		2 40		882	" Chinook... (Chief Joseph de- "	2410	882			3 11		f 9 02	f 9 02
	f 5 03				887	" Adams..... feated 1877) "	2423	878					8 55	
	5 10				891	" Lohman .... "	2445	874					f 8 45	f 8 45
	f 5 23				898	" Toledo (Bearpaw Mts. south) "	2467	867					Lv 8 30	
Lv 7 20	Ar 5 40	3 25	7 00		905	Ar Havre◆ (County Seat) Lv	2486	860	10 05	2 30		Ar 4 00	
f 7 30		3 45	7 15		905	Lv Havre◆ (Ft. Assini- Ar	2486	860	9 50	2 10		f 3 50	
f 7 42					909	" Pacific June ..boine 7 miles s.w.)	2550	856					f 3 31	
f 7 52					915	" Burnham	2633	850					3 22	
8 03					919	" Fresno	2690	846					f 3 12	
f 8 13					924	" Kremlin	2832	841					3 05	
8 20					930	" Xenia	2875	835					2 55	
8 31					934	" Gildford	2830	831					2 45	
8 42					940	" Hingham	3036	825					2 35	
8 55					946	" Rudyard	3112	819					2 25	
9 05					952	" Inverness	3306	813					f 2 17	
f 9 10					956	" Joplin	3307	809					2 05	
9 23		5 33			959	" Buelow	3415	806					f 1 53	
f 9 34					966	" Chester (County Seat)..	3139	799			12 20		1 40	
9 48					972	" Tiber	3191	793					1 27	
10 00					979	" Lothair(Sweet Grass Hills North)	3308	786					1 14	
10 13					985	" Galata	3096	780					f 1 05	
f10 21					991	" Devon (Summit of Rocky Mtns.	3114	771					f 1 05	
10 30					996	" Telstad ......100 mi. west)	3233	769					f12 58	
f10 40					1000	" Dunkirk	3304	765					f12 48	
Ar10 50					1005	" Farrell ......Oil fields north)	3380	759					Lv12 40	
	10 15	6 55	10 10		1009	**Shelby◆11, 65** (County Seat)	3280	756	7 08	11 08		6 30	
	f10 29				1017	" Simla	3469	748					f 6 10	
	10 39				1022	" Eldridge	3539	743					6 00	
	f10 52				1030	" Baltic	3886	735					f 5 50	
	11 00	7 45			1034	" Cut Bank (County Seat)	3740	731					f 5 40	
	f11 12				1039	" Gunsight	3931	725					f 5 27	
	f11 20				1043	" Sundance	3993	722					f 5 20	
	f11 32				1048	" Fort Piegan	3988	717					f 5 10	
	f11 45				1054	" Meriwether (Lewis Monu-	4080	711					f 5 00	
						ment. Farthest point north								
						reached by Lewis and								
						Clark in 1806)								
	12 01				1060	Ar Blackfoot (Chief Mtn. to Lv	4151	705		4 50				
	12 05				1060	Lv Blackfoot ... northwest) Ar	4151	705		4 45				
	12 30	8 52			1067	" Fort Browning (Blackfeet	4151	705						
						Indian Agency)								
	f12 40				1072	" Triple Divide	4466	698		9 27	4 25			
	f12 50					" Spotted Robe.......	4729	693			4 05			
	1 15	x 9 25	x12 17		1081	Ar Glacier Park◆11, 15 (Glacier	4901	689			f 3 55			
	f 1 22				1083	Lv Bison............ Park	4806	684	x 4 42	x 9 00	3 45			
	f 1 29				1086	" Rising Wolf ...... Hotel	4897	682			3 28			
	1 43				1093	" Summit (Continental..	5044	679			f 3 22			
						Divide, John F. Stevens	GLA-							
	f 1 59				1099	" Blacktail (Tunnel).. Status)	CIER 5213	672	3 10					
	f 2 09				1103	" Singleshot .... NA-	4664	666	f 2 50					
	f 2 20				1107	" Nimrod (Flathead Riv.) TION-	4396	662	2 40					
	2 31				1111	" Walton (Scalplock Mtn.) AL	4158	658	f 2 28					
	f 2 43				1116	" Pinnacle (Mt. St. Nich- PARK	3571	654	2 18					
						olas 9,385 ft.)	Open							
	f 2 55				1121	" Hidden Lake (Double June	3704	649	f 2 04					
	3 07				1125	" Red Eagle..... Mtn.) 15 in	3550	644	f 1 54					
	f 3 19				1132	" Silvertip .... Sept.	3360	638	1 42					
Motor	3 32	x11 21	x 2 33		1138	**Belton** (Belton Chalets) 15	3219	633	f 1 32					
263 Daily	3 07				1141	" Grizzly	3289	627	x 2 04	x 6 31	f 1 18		Motor	
	3 51				1146	" Citadel (Flathead River)	3288	624			f 1 09		**264** Daily	
Lv 8 23	4 10	11 54	3 03		1153	" Columbia Falls, 11, 66 (Flat-	3158	619	1 33	6 00	12 58		Ar 7 35	
						head River) Lv	3095	612			12 48			
7 40		6 35	12 30	3 40	1168	Ar Kalispell ◆66, 67....Lv	2959	626	12 50	5 15	11 15			
	2 25	11 15	2 25		1168	Lv Kalispell .... Ar	2959	626	2 10	6 35				
f 8 34	f 4 16				1156	Lv Half Moon (Lumber Mills) Ar	3079	609			f12 20		f 7 28	
8 45	Ar 4 25	12 10	3 15		1161	Lv **Whitefish◆** (Whitefish Lake) "	3040	604	1 05	5 40	f12 10		f 7 20	
8 50		12 20	3 25		1161	Lv **Whitefish 11** "	3040	604	1 05	5 30			7 15	
f 9 00					1166	" Vista............. Lv	3073	599					f 7 06	
f 9 14					1173	" Lupfer	3112	592					f 6 55	
f 9 25					1178	" Olney	3174	587					f 6 45	
f 9 38					1184	" Radnor	3211	581					f 6 34	
f 9 50					1191	" Stryker	3293	574					6 22	
f10 01					1197	" Trego (Wolf Mountains)	3308	568					f 6 08	

x Trains 1, 2, 3 and 4 stop at Glacier Park and Belton June 15 to Sept. 15.   ◆G. N. Restaurant.

Going-to-the-Sun Mountain Glacier National Park

Statue of John F. Stevens, at Summit

GREAT NORTHERN

TIME TABLES

The EMPIRE BUILDER ᷉ THE ORIENTAL LIMITED

JUNE, 1930

GLACIER NATIONAL PARK

Great Northern timetables were founts of information. Besides arrival and departure times, they included distance traveled, elevation, and details about scenic attractions en route. In this instance there's a promotion for Going-to-the-Sun Chalets and a photo of the recently erected statue to John F. Stevens, who is credited with "discovering" Marias Pass on a freezing day in December 1889.

ing the railway with just the four major hotels—Glacier Park Hotel, Many Glacier Hotel, Lake McDonald Hotel (which it operated for the Park Service), and the Prince of Wales Hotel—plus Swiftcurrent and Rising Sun motels. The only chalet that remained in the Great Northern's possession was Two Medicine, which was closed part by part until only the dining hall remained.

Louis Hill's death in 1948 freed Great Northern executives to pursue a new direction for the railway—one without the Glacier hotels. In the hands of a new president, John Budd, whose father Ralph had headed the railway a generation before, Great Northern officials were determined to get out of the hotel business. The problem was finding a taker.

Meanwhile, the railway displayed its obvious disinterest in the concession by refusing to take out long leases for the hotels, and ignoring pleas from the National Park Service to forge a long-term plan for them.

As far as the public was concerned, though, it was business as usual. "The feeling was that we better keep the hotels running in the traditional way as they were popular," said Robert Downing, executive vice-president of the Great Northern.

By 1951, only two percent of visitors to Glacier Park came by train; the rest arrived in private cars. "Today the Cads and Packards and smaller jobs flash along the highways in the paradisal mountainland, pause a night or so at one of the hotels or chalets and then go on to the Canadian or Pacific coast resorts, leaving little in the Glacier hotel company strong boxes," *Cut Bank Pioneer Press* columnist Dan Whetstone wrote. It's a "pretty thin" margin on which to run a hotel company that was open only sixty to eighty days each summer, he added.

The Great Northern's disenchantment rubbed off on other concessioners. Howard Hays, who had taken over Glacier Park Transport Company from Roe Emery in 1927, could see the end. In 1955, Hays sold his red buses to Glacier Park Company, as the hotel company had been renamed after the war, to make a better package for a future buyer. In 1938, Swanson had sold his interest in Swanson Boat Company to Arthur J. Burch of Kalispell, who reconstituted it as Glacier Park Boat Company. The saddle horse concession was shared among a number of small ranchers who divided up the park to suit their geographical locations. Day rides replaced extended saddle horse trips.

Despite its intention of divesting itself of the hotels and chalets, the Great Northern continued to operate them until 1956, when railway officials could no longer ignore another threat to its business. "It became apparent things would not grow," said Downing, referring to passenger traffic on the revamped *Empire Builder* and new *Western Star* trains. "Passenger travel by jets took off in 1958 and traffic on trains nosedived."

The railway turned over management of the hotel chain in 1957 to Donald T. Knutson, who ran a construction company in Minneapolis

The Empire Builder *was introduced in June 1929 as Great Northern's premier train on its 2,200-mile run from Chicago to Seattle. It featured all-new, heavyweight Pullman rolling stock—comfortable and quiet, and fully equipped with dining car, observation section, men's and women's dressing lounges, and a barbershop, to name a few of the amenities. Today the modern* Empire Builder, *owned and operated by Amtrak, is the only regularly scheduled passenger train outside Alaska to stop at a major U.S. national park.*

POST-WAR VACATION

**this
is the year
and this
the right train**

Seattle and Portland are only two nights from Chicago on Great Northern's swift, streamlined New Empire Builder. No extra fare.

Modern coaches with leg rests. No additional charge for reserved seats.

You enjoy privacy and restful sleep in luxurious duplex roomettes and bedrooms.

GREAT NORTHERN'S
NEW EMPIRE BUILDER

● This year visit the Pacific Northwest and California to your heart's content. Travel on the *first* and *finest* postwar transcontinental train. Diesel powered, this green and orange superliner streaks along the smoothest roadbed in the Northwest. Inside there's more color, more comfort, more convenience than you'd have thought possible before the war. Come aboard soon! Write to V. J. KENNY, Passenger Traffic Manager, Great Northern Railway, St. Paul 1, Minn.

The Great Northern's post–World War II efforts to increase train tourism to Glacier were futile, despite introduction of the stream-lined and, yet again, newly equipped Empire Builder in 1946. Park visitation grew markedly after the war, but that was due to private vehicles, improved roads and the opening of campgrounds and motels.

and owned hotels in Minnesota and North Dakota. As an enticement, the Great Northern agreed to spend $3 million over the three years (1957-1959) to renovate the chain, the idea being Knutson might buy the hotels at contract's end. What followed were some of the most extensive renovations seen at the hotels—upgrading services, creating convention facilities, and modernizing decor. Unfortunately, many distinct architectural features were destroyed, such as the loss of the double-helix staircase with its fountain at Many Glacier Hotel, and the grand staircase at the Prince of Wales Hotel. Knutson also removed many of the Indian artifacts commissioned by Hill to decorate the hotels, cutting long-standing ties to the Blood (in Alberta) and Blackfeet (in Montana) tribes whose members had created the pieces. Replacing native dancers and speakers, professional musicians were hired to perform in the hotel lobbies and newly opened liquor lounges, while reluctant staff was cajoled into putting on variety shows.

The Knutson experiment was considered a dismal failure, and he was not allowed to renew his contract or buy the properties; the Great Northern lost $1.5 million during Knutson's tenure. The Great Northern eventually found a suitable successor in Don Hummel, businessman, lawyer and, at the time, mayor of Tucson, Arizona. What set Hummel apart was his previous experience as a national parks concessioner, having built facilities in California's Lassen in 1933-1934, and later operated in Alaska's Mount McKinley and California's Yosemite. Hummel was also well connected in Washington, D.C.

Hummel was initially reluctant to take on the Glacier concession, particularly after seeing Great Northern's books and learning the railway had lost between $128,000 and $588,000 in each of the past five seasons. As with Louis Hill before him, Hummel was captivated by the scenery when he was finally persuaded to visit the park and, being an entrepreneur, he could imagine the potential. Hummel, his brother Gail, and Hummel's law school friend Don Ford formed Glacier Park Inc. and, after arranging payment of the $1.4-million price, assumed operation in December 1960.

Hummel attempted to take the Glacier hotels in a new direction. He was quick to note the trend of tour bus travel, which had been building since the late 1940s, with companies such as Greyhound, Tauck, and Cartan. Groups would fly to Calgary or Kalispell, and take a bus tour through the Rockies. Glacier Park Inc. also attempted to woo convention business, investing in renovations—expanding on designs started by Knutson. With conventions, Hummel hoped to increase occupancy during the shoulder seasons—June and September. The initiative for renovating came after a severe flood hit Glacier Park in 1964, damaging many facilities. Since repairs were required anyway, Hummel chose to launch some of his modernization and upgrades then, with insurance picking up part of the tab.

While Hummel was roundly respected as a leader among national park concessioners, he was viewed by some as an old-style operator, his desire for a viable commercial operation pitting him against others who focused on conservation. His sometimes brusque and outspoken manner caused considerable friction, finally alienating him from fellow concessioners and federal administrators. After nearly two decades of running battles with the National Park Service reminiscent of those between the service and Louis Hill, Hummel sold Glacier Park Inc. to Greyhound Food Management of Phoenix, Arizona, in March 1981. As Glacier Park, Inc., it is now a division of Viad Corp of Phoenix.

Today, the legacy of Great Northern Railway hotels and chalets remains. They are split up, with little chance the empire will ever be rejoined, but they survive as notable and enduring features of the landscape of the Glacier Park region. Each one has received some form of national historic designation or recognition.

Come with us now as we go back to the time of Louis Hill and Great Northern Railway to explore the origin of each building, how they operated, who visited them, and what has happened to them since.

Eugenia (Genee) and Don Hummel. Don, with other partners, created Glacier Park Inc. in 1960 to take over Great Northern's accommodations in the park. A lawyer in Arizona before World War II, Don Hummel had served with distinction as a lieutenant colonel in the air force, receiving the Bronze Star, Legion of Merit and two Chinese government awards. He and Genee were married in 1947. Hummel's involvement in national parks concessions began in Lassen in 1933.

J.J. Hill's seventy-fifth-birthday party at Glacier Park Hotel hosted some 600 people, most of whom arrived on special trains for the September 16, 1913, gala. The banquet to honor "The Empire Builder" was so large the lobby had to be used to accommodate the diners. Revelers enjoyed "Going-to-the-Sun" canapés with dry martinis, followed by mountain trout meuniere and Parisienne potatoes served with claret, and a main course of Montana beef tenderloin with fresh mushrooms, stuffed bell peppers, "Glacier salad," and Champagne.

— Chapter 2 —

Glacier Park Lodge

Glacier Park Lodge is not the biggest in the chain of hotels and chalets that the Great Northern built to serve Glacier National Park nor was it the first constructed, but as the "entrance hotel" it was the most important. When railway was the king of transportation and the only easy way to reach the park, Glacier Park Hotel (its name until the late 1950s) was the start and end point for most packaged tours. Its design, appointments, and service set the tone for the experience travelers could expect, and managers went out of their way to ensure guests were as happy when they left as when they arrived. It's a role that hasn't changed since the June day the hotel opened in 1913; it still serves as gatekeeper for the park, and headquarters for the hotels.

RAY DJUFF COLLECTION

Few people realize that 155-room Glacier Park Lodge and the neighboring community of East Glacier Park are within the Blackfeet Indian Reservation, and not the park proper. The townsite, originally called Midvale, was a relatively obscure siding on the Great Northern's mainline, 1,500 miles from Chicago to the east, and 700 miles from Seattle to the west. The decision to locate the railway's head-quarters hotel in Midvale was not wholly up to Louis Hill. By the time Glacier became a national park in 1910, there was already a thriving tourism business around Lake McDonald, west of the Continental Divide. The only area of the park that had not been staked out was the eastern slopes of the Rockies, and Midvale—population 100—was the closest access point.

Initially Hill thought he'd be able to buy an existing plot, but the Department of the Interior informed him "no land has been set aside in the town plan for a hotel and the land is not for sale." That didn't stop Hill. Using personal influence, he had Montana Senator Joseph M. Dixon push a bill through Congress to sell him 160 acres of land on the reserve. It passed in February 1912. Even so, Hill ran into problems. While the bill suggested a price of $25 an acre, the Indian agent would

Glacier Park Annex Track Side 31 Jan. 1914

Boxcars filled with lumber and other building supplies wait on a spur line to be unloaded during construction of Glacier Park Hotel's bedroom annex over the winter of 1913-1914. The outside columns of the annex are cedar, better to withstand the weather, while those on the inside are Douglas-fir. Each of the large columns is thirty-six to 40 inches in diameter. Only two or three would fit on each flat car on the trip from the Pacific Northwest, where the 500- to 800-year-old trees were harvested.

not sell it to Hill for less than $90. Upset, Hill suggested publicly that he was looking into an alternate site two miles away, just outside the reserve. He then secretly organized a protest by area residents, who sent telegrams to Senator Dixon, who then waved them menacingly at Department of the Interior officials. The ruse worked, and the price was dropped to $30 an acre. "The agent made an error," Hill was informed.

So in March 1912, with the contract let to E.G. Evensta and Company of Minneapolis, work began on the hotel site by creating a camp for workers, and staking out the building's location.

Louis Hill had a definite vision of what he wanted for his entrance hotel. It had to be big, massive to the point of surpassing every natural and man-made object in the vicinity. The eastern entrance of Glacier Park had to tweak visitors' imaginations and desire to explore and see the wonders beyond. Hill chose as the model for the entrance hotel the Forestry Building constructed for the 1905 Lewis and Clark Centennial Exposition in Portland, Oregon. He ordered a set of blueprints for his architect, Samuel H. Bartlett of St. Paul.

The Forestry Building was billed as the world's largest log cabin. It took the humble building that had served America's frontier forefathers and transformed it into a monumental structure. Architects picked up on the style, mimicking the post and beam construction, adding fancy scrollwork on window and door frames. This latter detail came from Swiss styles, which particularly interested Hill. He asked a bookstore in

St. Paul to find as many titles on Swiss architecture as it could and, after perusing them, Hill forwarded the tomes (*Der Schweizer Holzstyl, Old Wood Architecture in Switzerland, Charakteristiche Holzbauten der Schweiz*) to Bartlett as possible inspiration. Bartlett worked on the design over the winter of 1911-1912 in preparation for beginning construction the following spring.

Hill took personal interest in every detail of the hotel, often with an eye on price and quality. He had hoped the contractor could use timber from the forestry district between Essex and Belton. When the stumpage fee proved more than Hill was willing to pay, he had Bartlett change the design to replace log walls with stud framing and exterior shakes, which could be produced cheaply by Great Northern's mill in Somers, Montana.

Hill's involvement sometimes caused confusion. When he saw that fieldstones had been planned for the foundation, he asked why. Chief engineer Albert Hogeland explained that's what Bartlett thought Hill wanted. Hill replied it was a misunderstanding, and all he wanted was rough concrete.

Glacier Park Hotel was opened on Sunday, June 15, 1913. There was no party to mark the occasion; guests simply started arriving. The Great Northern had planned to run a special excursion train from Kalispell and Columbia Falls for an opening day party, but hotel manager J.M. Cathcart postponed it at the last minute. Hotel staff wouldn't arrive until

Although the furnishings and telephone have changed since this 1913 photo was taken, the character of bedrooms at Glacier Park Lodge remains much the same to this day. The raised floor in the bathroom was created as an easy way to reach pipes that had to be drained at the end of each summer to prevent freezing, because the building is unheated all winter. Pure wool blankets supplemented steam heating during the season.

Above: *The head on the U.S. nickel issued in March 1913, just before Glacier Park Hotel opened, bore a striking resemblance to that of Two Guns White Calf (above), a Blackfeet chief. Some 1.2 billion Indian head/ buffalo nickels were minted until 1937, each one an advertisement for White Calf and Glacier Park.*

Below: *The Glacier Park Hotel's basement "plunge pool" was innovative for its time and provided curative benefits for guests who had spent a day on the trail—whether afoot or on horseback.*

the night before, and Cathcart "wanted to give excursionists the very best entertainment."

The event was delayed until June 22, with 260 people enjoying tours of the grounds, a free meal at the hotel, entertainment by local Blackfeet, and dancing to music by the Kalispell Elks Club band.

Hill and the Great Northern went on a promotional frenzy. "The White Men are Coming. Come this season. America's newest and grandest scenic playground—awaits you!" read advertisements in newspapers and magazines. "A magnificent new hotel, one of the most novel and interesting institutions of its kind in the country, has just been completed. Every room is electrically lighted and [steam] heated. Every modern feature including shower baths and plunge pool, has been installed. The cuisine is worthy of the finest eastern establishments. The rates— American plan $2 to $5 a day. Tours through Glacier Park by automobile, horseback, launch, stage and afoot—$1 to $5 per day."

Hill got into the act personally on several fronts. When the new Indian head/buffalo nickel entered circulation in 1913, he sent a memo to his advertising agent suggesting a news story on the "new 'See America First' Glacier Park nickel, with profile of [Two Guns] White Calf." White Calf, a prominent Blackfeet chief, bore an uncanny resemblance to the native on the nickel. While White Calf wasn't one of the models for the coin, it helped Great Northern's cause that the designer, James Earle Fraser, couldn't remember the names of the three Indians he used for the composite drawing.

Probably Hill's greatest promotional coup in 1913, though, was to sponsor the Glidden Tour, a nationally known automobile endurance test. Charles J. Glidden, a retired New England telephone magnate and automobile enthusiast, had started the tour but by 1912 it had waned, and the scheduled run from Detroit to New Orleans failed to materialize. That's when Hill stepped in, offering support for a 1,245-mile, nine-day Twin City–Glacier Park tour for 1913. The route paralleled

Great Northern's line, and drivers were followed by a special "hotel" train where they could sleep, eat meals, and have their cars fixed—and from which the accompanying press corps issued bulletins to their papers. There was also a press car, containing a Linotype machine, a photo-engraving plant, and mail facilities, that produced a daily bulletin for the racers and for distribution in towns through which they passed.

The awards dinner at Glacier Park Hotel, at which the Glidden Cup was handed to the Metz team, was a symbolic moment. The last of the Glidden Tours marked the second arrival of auto-travelers to Glacier from the Midwest (the first had been the previous year at Belton). It was the beginning of a trend that would decades later scuttle rail passenger traffic to Glacier as a viable source of revenue for the Great Northern, and end the railway's hotel and chalet ownership.

As a grand finale for the 1913 season, Louis Hill and the members of the railway veterans' association arranged a seventy-fifth birthday party for J.J. Hill at Glacier Park Hotel. All of J.J. Hill's old friends were invited to the September 16 gala, including every Great Northern engineer, conductor, brakeman, and station agent who had served with the company for twenty-five years or more. In all, about 600 people attended,

The members of the Great Northern veterans association presented railway founder J.J. Hill and his wife Mary with seventy-five American roses during the September 1913 seventy-fifth birthday party for the "Empire Builder" at Glacier Park Hotel. It's very likely the flowers were brought in from one of the railway's greenhouses in Washington state, which were used to supply most of the horticultural needs of the hotel and chalet operations in Glacier.

608 - Flower Beds at Hotel - Glacier Park, Montana.

This was the sight that greeted tourists when they got off the train at Glacier Park Station. Selected members of the Blackfeet tribe were invited to set up their teepees on the hotel grounds. Walking to the hotel, tourists also got to inspect the 22,000 square-foot flower bed that featured up to 100 species of perennials and annuals. Louis Hill personally directed the work of the hotel gardeners, selecting the plants, bulbs, and seed, and planning their arrangements.

the partygoers arriving on special trains. The celebration was one of the largest held in the Northwest, and would be talked about in railway circles for years to come.

It was a gala ending to what had been an incredibly successful first season for the Great Northern's hotels and chalets. The traveling public's reaction was overwhelmingly positive, although not everyone agreed with the "sight-seeing assembly line" Louis Hill had created. "I was whirled about in motor cars which seemed an affront to the former sanctity of those mountains; [forced] to submit to being conducted by licensed guides over trails which I had myself discovered and made; in short everything was done to make us feel that the wilderness with its Indians had gone and modern American tourism had taken its place," said Henry L. Stimson, twice Secretary of War and a man who had trekked Glacier trails for twenty-one years prior to Hill's tourism machine.

Hill began laying plans for further expansion. At Glacier Park Hotel he ordered construction of a bedroom annex as big again as the lobby section. Evensta was handed the cost-plus contract and began work almost immediately after the hotel's doors closed for the 1913 season. With the addition of the "bridge" and 111-bedroom annex, the entire Glacier Park Hotel complex cost the railway $786,226.67.

Glacier Park Hotel was the great crossroads for Glacier Park. Tourists passed through Glacier Park Hotel by the thousands, an untold number arriving by automobile, and as many as 9,000 a year on scheduled railway tours.

One of the great expectations of tourists coming to Glacier was to meet Blackfeet natives, and the Great Northern did not disappoint, paying selected members of the tribe to dance, sing, and demonstrate skills for visitors. "Among the older Indians, who pitch their teepees in the vicinity of the Glacier Park Hotel during the summer, the memory of great buffalo hunts, inter-tribal strife, fur-trading and horse stealing are still alive," Great Northern brochures touted. "Stories of the old days,

ceremonial songs and dances, feature the Indian pow-wows at which the Glacier Park visitors are always welcome." In their buckskin regalia, the Indians "frightened me a bit as a 10-year-old," said Howard (Tim) Hays Jr. of Riverside, Calif.

For a select few, usually dignitaries, the railway paid natives to induct them into the Blackfeet tribe. The railway paid for headdresses and gifts presented. Local and national media invariably covered the ceremonies and the ever-growing membership in the "white Blackfeet" guaranteed the railway continuing nationwide publicity. The "white Blackfeet" tribe included: President Franklin and Eleanor Roosevelt; William Gibbs McAdoo, director general of the railroad administration; actor Clark Gable; FBI boss J. Edgar Hoover; Norway's Crown Prince Olav and Princess Martha; and Secretary of the Interior Harold Ickes.

In the early years, Hill wanted to be informed of all important visitors to Glacier, and would sometimes be at Glacier Park Hotel to personally greet them. Detailed lists of VIPs were kept. "Mrs. John Fletcher and party of friends from Chicago. This lady is the wife of the vice-president of Ford, Dearborn, National Bank of Chicago," read one such note. In case hotel managers or staff missed the notices, Hill would also write a letter of introduction to be presented to hotel and chalet managers, ensuring the party received proper treatment.

Blackfeet Indians regularly met the train at the depot, posing for pictures and adding to the atmosphere. In the evenings, a group of Blackfeet gave demonstrations in the hotel lobby, which included dancing, drumming and singing. Special visiting dignitaries were inducted into the Blackfeet tribe; **below,** *Princess Martha of Norway is so honored during a June 1939 visit.*

Adolph Heinz was one of a bevy of artists, mostly German, commissioned by Louis Hill to produce works used to promote Glacier Park. Here, Heinz paints Granite Park Chalets and Heaven's Peak, a scene that was used for the railway's May 1929 calendar. Railway officials were disappointed in the quality of reproduction of Heinz's landscapes and eventually quit using them in favor of Indian portraits by Winold Reiss.

A talented amateur artist himself, Hill recognized the value of paintings in promoting Glacier, and for years staff at Glacier Park Hotel saw a stream of artists come through the doors. It started with the hiring of Austrian-born artist John Fery to paint vast panoramic landscapes of the park for the railway's "See America First" campaign. He was followed by Julius Seyler (distantly connected to Louis Hill by marriage); W. Langdon Kihn; Kathryn Woodman Leighton to produce pictures of Blackfeet elders used in a lecture series; Adolph Heinz to do park landscapes; and Winold Reiss.

Reiss became a favorite of Hill and, in 1927 and 1928, the German-born artist had a studio in the hotel's basement, where he painted portraits of Blackfeet and local pioneers. Agnes Clarke Judge, daughter of Midvale founder Horace Clarke, was one those models, her image ending up on a postcard. Posing for a Reiss painting was "big money," said Judge, also known by her Blackfeet name Morning Star. Reiss paid $5 an hour for sittings lasting two hours a day over the period of several weeks. "He was very interesting," she said. "He told me about his life in New York and all over."

Staff at Glacier Park Hotel saw more of Hill than workers at any other location because they were on the railway's mainline—a quick stop on Hill's frequent cross-country business trips. One person sure to run for cover at the mention of Hill's impending arrival was the groundskeeper. Hill was an avid gardener, and wanted to ensure the hotel and its surroundings made a proper first impression. He selected the irises, gladioli, and peonies himself, usually in Spokane, and then provided the gardener, in the early years George Dishmaker, with detailed instructions for handling.

"Advise me as soon as the bulbs arrive," Hill demanded. "I would like to have these planted around the border and around in the flower beds near the big hotel," Hill said in another missive. "There are a number of annual stocks, also, that might be well to plant right close to the hotel by the porch. These should go in the ground as soon as possible as it is already a little late for moving them."

Mike's Place was both figuratively and literally "across the tracks" from Glacier Park Station and the hotel. Here hotel staff, wranglers and bus drivers could let their hair down in an atmosphere that was both festive and relaxed. Mike's Place, named for owner Mike Shannon, was such a popular community center that it was rebuilt almost immediately after being destroyed in a 1924 fire.

The favorite retreat of Glacier Park Hotel staff from Hill and other managers was Mike's Place, a combination dance hall, restaurant/soda fountain and pool hall whose art deco facade dominated the main street of Midvale. There, staff traded tales about the day's events with cowboys from the Park Saddle Horse Company corrals, drivers and mechanics from the Glacier Park Transportation Company garages, railway employees, and even "dudes" looking for someplace less formal than the hotel to hang out.

Problems at the U.S.-Canada border were a common cause of complaint after the opening of the Prince of Wales Hotel in Waterton Park, in 1927. Canada has strict laws prohibiting handgun importation, and the customs inspector at the Prince of Wales had the unpleasant and not always easy duty of confiscating the weapons. To avoid the situation, Glacier Park Hotel employees began warning guests about Canada's gun laws, which led to the practice of guests having the hotel's mail clerk package and send the gun to the owner's home. The practice lasted for decades, until the U.S. Postal Service learned about the guns and ammunition it was unknowingly toting from Glacier Park. "If it is necessary to accept packages containing guns," the hotel company informed its employees, "they must be accepted for shipment by express."

On rare occasions, Mike's Place became a source of manpower for the hotel when it was short-staffed, particularly at the end of the season. The untrained workers pulled from Mike's Place elsewhere in Midvale could lead to unexpected situations.

Jack Brewster recalled one year when Glacier Park Hotel was closing

Ralph Budd became railway president in 1919, having been groomed for the job by James J. Hill. With Budd as president, Louis Hill had more time to attend to his role as chairman of the board. According to historian Michael Malone, Budd "would become perhaps the most prestigious of all Hill's proteges, a key railroad leader of the next generation."

September 15, most of the staff had been let go except for a skeleton crew, and managers realized they had a party booked for September 17 and 18. "My brother and I and two Indian boys took the job on as bellhops," Brewster said. "The first night after things quieted down, they gave us two baskets to go around to the rooms and pick up the shoes and clean them. Nobody told us the pencil and white card were to mark the room number down. We ended up with two baskets of shoes and no room numbers." It was a hilarious sight, Brewster said, to see all those tourists in their stocking feet milling around the lobby trying to sort out what shoes belonged to whom.

Incidents like that were anathema to hotel company officials. General manager Howard Noble noted in a memo to hotel managers that "out of 6,000 letters sent to guests that were there last year [1927], only two came back with criticisms. Most of them praised our service and the park." He added: "We have the report of the best service in any park except Grand Canyon. Let's make it better than that—so good they can't catch up with us."

In the hotel company's ever-continuing search for new ways to please guests, managers came up with the idea of adding a nine-hole golf course at Glacier Park Hotel. Tourists, they concluded, were too eager to leave the hotel to explore the interior of Glacier Park. A golf course "would eventually be one of the biggest attractions to hold people at this hotel that we could possibly inaugurate," said Noble. There was an ulterior motive to building the course: In buying 1,000 acres to add to the 180 the railway already owned, "we would be fairly well protected from the building of undesirable and unsightly structures and the encroachment of undesirable people directly against our premises," railway president Ralph Budd noted. The land purchases topped $80,000.

Construction of the course turned into a mild fiasco for the hotel company. Work began in the spring of 1927 and quickly fell behind schedule. The contractor, William H. Tucker and Sons, Inc. of New York, complained of not having enough workers and not receiving requested equipment. Problems continued throughout the summer, with reports that the contractor and his foreman were "unreliable" and a "bad influence on the Great Northern." Finally, Louis Hill could stand the delays no longer and fired the contractor—the job unfinished. Dishmaker, the ever-burdened gardener, was ordered to oversee completion. The nine-hole course was the first in the state to offer grass greens.

The golf course, supplemented by putting green, tennis court, bowling green, and croquet grounds, was no match for the Great Depression of the 1930s. Great Northern officials discussed building a motel at

Midvale to get business from economy-minded car tourists, but never followed through.

It was a tumultuous time for both the railway and the hotel company, with Louis Hill stepping down as chairman of the board in 1929, and no longer providing guidance and advice. At the hotel company, Howard Noble retired after forty-two years of service with the railway, replaced, after some dallying by senior railway officials, by A.J. Binder. Binder lasted until 1934, when Adolph Aszmann took over.

Glacier Park Hotel got a much-needed boost during the Depression when it hosted the ceremony that joined Glacier and Waterton as the world's first international peace park. The idea originated at an international Rotary Club meeting the previous summer at the Prince of Wales

Thirteen years of on-again, off-again discussions took place before the golf course at Glacier Park Hotel was built within the boundary of the Blackfeet Indian Reservation. Originally intended to be eighteen holes, it was completed as a par-thirty-six, nine-hole course. For a time, hotel employees were prohibited from playing here because the "high class guests prefer not to play on the same course with employees." Greens fees were $1 per round and included a shower and use of the "plunge pool." The course is still in use, with each hole named for a historical chief of the Blackfeet nation.

Hotel, as a way to mark the long history of good relations between Canada and the United States. Rotarians initially thought the June 18, 1932, ceremony linking the two parks in a non-administrative union wouldn't happen because of delays in Canada's Parliament, which didn't pass the act until late May. The preparations were necessarily hurried.

The spectacle began with Chief Two Guns White Calf giving a sign talk translated by Richard Sanderville, followed by speeches by Bear Track of the Salish tribe, and Loose Moccasin Grizzly Bear of the Kootenai tribe. Messages were read from President Herbert Hoover and Canadian Prime Minister R.B. Bennett, and then a bronze tablet on a cairn between the hotel and Glacier Park Station was unveiled by Canon Samuel H. Middleton, a Rotarian from Cardston, Alberta, who had been the prime mover for the peace park initiative. It was a suitably elaborate ceremony filled with allusion and symbolism, marking what has become an enduring international movement.

President Franklin D. Roosevelt's tour over Going-to-the-Sun Highway in 1934 was another cause for hope, as were the lifting of Prohibition and opening of a bar at Glacier Park Hotel that same year.

The dining room at Glacier Park Hotel featured hostesses in native and oriental garb, as shown in this 1930 photo. The waitresses' Swiss costumes remained in use until the late-1930s, with minor changes over the years. Here, the waitresses wear the "slippers" later replaced by a stiff oxford that many servers found uncomfortable.

Although pleased to have had his touring cars and buses used by the presidential retinue, Howard Hays, head of Glacier Park Transport Company, was not always thrilled with all the Roosevelt administration's policies. "I recall that my father was exasperated by the NRA [National Recovery Act]," said William Hays, Howard Hays's son. "If an employee lifted one finger outside of his specified hours, his/her employer was in trouble with the federal government."

A rising militancy in the hotel company's workforce was also evident. In 1937, a group of waitresses revolted when the "slippers" that had been part of their uniform for years were replaced by thick-soled, stiff, black oxfords. They laid out their concerns on the back of a menu sent to Aszmann: "No perforations in shoes. Too thick and uncomfortable. Warm," signed Barbara Hall. "I don't think everyone is fitted to the same style of shoe. I'd much prefer another style," signed Elizabeth Tagan. "They're very stiff. I'm having difficulty standing on my feet for any length of time," signed Corine Carlson. Not only did Aszmann reject their complaints, he also raised the deposit on waitress uniforms from $10 to $11.50, due to the oxfords' higher price.

When war broke out in Europe in 1939, the hotel company went from having a surplus of available employees to trying to find enough to fill vacancies. Young men and women found better paying jobs in war work or by joining the military. "Most of the drivers were registered with the draft boards at home," said gear-jammer (staff slang for bus driver) Herman Rusch of Plymouth, Minnesota. "We expected to be drafted. Some young men went to Canada and enlisted or went to Toronto and hid out." In 1942 the hotel company posted signs at all its front desks apologizing to guests for poor service due to lack of manpower.

Glacier Park Hotel, like most of the rest in Great Northern's chain in Glacier Park, was not opened in 1943 due to travel restrictions. It remained closed until the summer of 1946. Heading the hotel company after the war was Joseph S. Jeffries, a long-time Great Northern employee. Jeffries had the unenviable task of shepherding Glacier Park

Hotel and the rest of the chain through a post-war period of change (rise of bus tours, decline of rail tours despite introduction of new trains, end of Park Saddle Horse concession, and takeover of the bus company) and removing or selling remote chalets. The glory years of the 1910s and 1920s were a fading memory, and railway executives were desperate to get out of the hotel business.

The staff at Glacier Park Hotel soldiered on, with Jeffries and hotel manager Andrew A. Roubek insisting on the same standards as before the war, although some sliding occurred on maintenance as budgets were trimmed. It took all the ingenuity Cy Stevenson, the head of maintenance for the hotel company, could muster to keep the building in tiptop shape so that the railway could continue to show off its premier hotel to such dignitaries as U.S. Chief Justice Earl Warren; Victor Mature, Vincent Price, William Bendix, and Piper Laurie; there to film

The decorations around the front desk of Glacier Park Hotel illustrate the lobby's hodgepodge of styles. The animal skins, mounted heads and bison skulls on the pillars were reflective of the Blackfeet, but the lobby also featured Navaho rugs and totem poles, used by West Coast tribes, by the main doorway (see photo on page 4). Oriental lanterns were a nod to the railway's links to Asia: its premier train was called the Oriental Limited, *and the railway's Great Northern Steamship Company ran the steamers* Minnesota *and* Dakota *between Seattle and Japan from 1905 to 1915.*

41

Above: *Joseph S. Jeffries.*

Below: *Oil paintings ringed the Glacier Park Hotel dining room, offering guests a glimpse of the sites they'd soon see or reminding them of where they'd been. Meals were included in the price of a vacation tour, with meal tickets issued so visitors did not have to carry much cash.*

Dangerous Mission; and Ronald Reagan and Barbara Stanwyck, who came to make the movie *Cattle Queen of Montana*.

Glacier Park Hotel, which had not undergone major changes since opening in 1913, got a needed shot in the arm in terms of maintenance during the Knutson years, 1957-1959. Some upgrades, such as baths and lavatories in every room, were long overdue. In updating the decor and entertainment, though, Knutson eliminated most links to the Blackfeet. Pictographs were removed and replaced with wallpaper, animal heads were taken down and pelts on balcony railings removed. Professional musicians and singers replaced native entertainers, and the lobby area where the Blackfeet had appeared became a cocktail lounge. Knutson also changed the name of the hotel to Glacier Park Lodge, a better moniker, he thought, for the remodeled building.

What man has created nature can take away in the blink of an eye, and Don Hummel feared the worst in June 1964 when Glacier Park was hit by the severest flooding in living memory. Fortunately the hotel was unharmed, but its water supply was knocked out for several days. Hummel also had to contend with hundreds of students arriving to take up summer jobs. The lodge became disaster central, with employees occupying guest rooms as opening for the season was more than a week away.

"Each evening I assembled all our employees and gave them the latest news," Hummel said. "On the third evening I had bad news. I would be unable to pay anyone until we could get the facilities open and establish a cash flow. I promised everyone room and board without charge. I offered all an opportunity to leave without any reflection on their employment records. Not a single employee left." It was a moment of pride in his staff for Hummel, one unmatched during his twenty-year ownership of the hotel chain.

Hummel sold Glacier Park Inc. in 1981, and Glacier Park Lodge changed hands for only the second time in its then nearly seventy-year history. The new owners have strived to maintain the legacy of the Great Northern Railway. Some surface features have been modernized, of course—such as computers at the front desk, a vastly larger and brighter gift shop, electric heaters to replace the steam heating in guest rooms, and a big-screen satellite television in The Lounge—but the essence of what tourists saw in June 1913 still stands. In 1999, *USA Today* named it one of the ten best lodges in America's national park system.

For those with a hankering, Amtrak's Chicago to Seattle passenger train, the *Empire Builder*, stops at the same Glacier Park Station where Great Northern's *Oriental Limited* first did ninety years before. And when visitors stand at the station staring down the walk to Glacier Park Lodge, it's almost as if time has stood still.

The twelve-foot-square, steel-hooded "camp fire" in the lobby of Glacier Park Hotel provided a relaxing gathering place. Rocking Windsor chairs added to the coziness. Later, the potential of a building fire forced removal of the camp circle. Louis Hill, very aware of fire danger, demanded that staff regularly hold fire drills.

This mid-1930s scene of Two Medicine Chalets illustrates the picturesque, planned layout of the colony, with Mount Sinopah standing tall as the significant landmark. The dining hall and kitchen, the only building that now remains, is on the extreme right. Beside it is one of two small guest cabins. Behind the departing touring car is the two-story chalet and, hidden in the trees on the extreme left, is the guest dormitory chalet.

— *Chapter 3* —

Two Medicine Chalets

Today for the first time in my life I have seen Glacier Park. Perhaps I can best express to you my thrill and delight by saying that I wish every American, both old and young, could have been with me today. The great mountains, the glaciers, the lakes and the trees make me long to stay for the rest of the summer.

—Franklin Delano Roosevelt
August 5, 1934

During President Franklin D. Roosevelt and his family's visit, they were entertained by a forty-man Civilian Conservation Corps chorus as well as by thirty Blackfeet who gave dances and demonstrations. The presidential party, including White House staff, Secret Service, park officials, concession owners and a battery of media representatives, required fourteen large touring cars.

The president's heartfelt words, spoken in a nationwide broadcast from Two Medicine Chalets, expressed the sentiments of many Glacier National Park visitors—those who had come before, and those who would follow. The splendor of the Two Medicine Valley is timeless. The valley has every natural feature a visitor could hope for: three pristine lakes in a chain, nearby waterfalls, all surrounded by "a dozen splendid mountains of which Rising Wolf, with its red [argillite] top of 9,510 feet, easily is the monarch."

As beautiful as it is, Louis Hill decided the valley needed "improvements" before tourists could enjoy the view. Hill chose Two Medicine for a chalet colony not only for its natural attractions, but also for its proximity to Glacier Park Hotel. Two Medicine Lake was an inviting destination where visitors could sate their appetite in the feast of nature's offerings, and quickly return to "civilization," a mere ten miles away.

The first tourist development at Two Medicine was a teepee camp established in 1911. Each tent had a wooden floor, cots, and a washstand. Guests were charged fifty cents a night, and took their meals in a rustic 18-by-60-foot log dining hall and kitchen, the first permanent structure built at the site.

There was no riding trail to Two Medicine in 1911. The wagon road had been "improved" by contractors hired by the Great Northern that summer, but was still primitive, offering a dusty and jerky ride for those in one of the Brewster brothers' four-horse stagecoaches. The fine network of well-kept hiking and riding trails that today radiate from Two

This line of tents for a private party, camping near Two Medicine, is reflective of the tent camps run by William Hilligoss and Great Northern. Promotional literature boasted: "In these camps is real comfort and abundance of mountain-climbing food at ordinary hotel prices."

Medicine weren't yet on the map; anyone heading out by foot or on horseback had to be prepared to bushwhack.

Sleeping in the teepees, tourists could imagine the Native American history of Two Medicine and, around the nightly campfires, they learned how the valley got its unusual name. There are many variations of the story, but all include the presence of double medicine lodges set up by separate Blackfeet clans for a religious ceremony known as the Okan, or Sun Dance.

In 1912, two log chalets were added. The budding resort attracted 389 guests its second season. For 1913, Hill boosted the size of the colony again, this time in readiness for the opening of Glacier Park Hotel and an expected onslaught of visitors. Added were a two-story, 28-foot-square cabin, and a 28-by-84-foot "dormitory," bringing to 146 the number of overnight guests that could be accommodated—one hundred in rooms and forty-six in the teepee camp. With considerable foresight, Hill insisted that the buildings be arranged along the lakeshore to give the impression of an enclave rather than random structures.

The two-story cabin had an ingenious arrangement of inside walls on the upper floors to circulate air through the building. Room partitions did not reach the ceiling, so that on chilly evenings heat from the fireplace could better flow to all rooms. What was not taken into consideration was the problem of those who snored or talked in their sleep.

In anticipation of completing the Mount Henry trail from Glacier Park Hotel (the first leg of what in 1915 would become the Inside Trail

saddle horse tour), Great Northern replaced the dining room/kitchen at Two Medicine with a larger, more elaborate building. Samuel Bartlett, who had designed Glacier Park Hotel, was given the job of drawing the plans for the 42-by-85-foot structure. The $10,876 contract went to James Brown.

The general ambiance at the chalets in the early years was one of relaxed country living.

"An after-dinner stroll took us to the chalets where we found a warm welcome," the diarist for the Seattle Mountaineers wrote of their 1914 visit. "In fact one of the charms of Glacier National Park is the air of hospitality that pervades it. Each feels himself an honored guest and the Mountaineers availed themselves of the opportunity to write letters and postcards, to enjoy refreshments served on real tables and from the broad verandah to watch the sunlight set on the lake."

The colony had the luxury of telephone communication with Glacier Park Hotel, electricity provided by an on-site generator, and cold running water in all rooms. "The boy will bring hot water on request." A central toilet/laundry building provided washrooms and hot baths. Besides fishing, boating, hiking and trail rides, guests found a croquet ground.

The accommodations may have been rustic, but what they lacked in amenities was made up for by spotless rooms with soft beds and warm woolen blankets, great service and excellent meals in the dining room— "artistic crudeness with comfort," as one railway brochure described it.

The two-story guest dormitory constructed at Two Medicine in 1913 featured twenty sleeping rooms and two lounging rooms. Separate buildings for men and women provided toilets, hot showers and baths. Following Swiss style, the roof featured log poles against which large stones were placed to keep the roof from being blown away by high winds.

Above: *Waitress Clista Wood.*

Below: *Sleeping quarters at Two Medicine were simple, clean and comfortable. This mid-1930s view shows the bedrooms of a cabin after modernization. Each bed was made with a warm Hudson Bay blanket. Extra blankets were available when it was cold, because heat came only from a central wood stove that guests had to stoke themselves. The railway described Two Medicine's rustic amenities as "relaxed country living."*

Maintaining the standards the hotel company wanted was no easy task for staff. The waitresses were expected to be as professional as at any eastern city establishment where menus were "called" rather than printed, and orders were taken without being written down.

"You can imagine how hard it was to keep everything straight for a table of six, for instance," said Clista Wood of Kalispell, Montana, a waitress at Two Medicine. "Breakfast was the worst as there were so many choices. I remember one young man who ordered so much that I finally stopped listening and brought him some of everything."

Besides waiting tables, Wood was called on to clear tables, wash dishes, and clean rooms. "It turned out to be the hardest physical labor I've ever done, and also the job with the longest hours," Wood said. "We were waitresses, we washed glasses and silver, made lunches for the 'dudes' who were going hiking or horseback riding, and made all the salads. When we finished our breakfast duties we became chambermaids, and I mean that in the literal sense; we emptied chamber pots (ugh) as well as the usual hotel maid jobs."

After dinner in the evenings, "those of us with any kind of talent entertained....We frequently worked from six in the morning until eight or nine at night," for which the staff got off one day a week.

The chalet manager was expected to overlook nothing and if he did, Louis Hill, on his regular forays to Glacier, would be sure to point them out. "The Two Medicine camp does not have fresh vegetables, cheese, pork or mutton," Hill once wrote, adding, "The camp also needs new curtains." His instructions were always detailed: "We should try to get a creosote that, when applied and dry, will shine like a spar varnish....I wish you would impress upon whoever undertakes the work that staining for appearance should not be considered; we want preservative for the wood; the appearance will be satisfactory."

Over time, the amenities for tourists at Two Medicine were expanded. One of the most notable was the addition of the 38-foot, forty-passenger tour boat *Rising Wolf.* The railway commissioned Captain William Swanson to build and operate *Rising Wolf,* which would lead to his capturing the boat concession licence on the park's east side and developing his own business.

The boat tours, trail rides, and other services at Two Medicine were also a

draw to through-train passengers who were given stop-over privileges during the summer at no extra charge. Two Medicine was possibly the most popular side trip for people with only a day to spare. Train travelers took the 1½-hour automobile journey from the station ($2.50 round trip), had lunch at Two Medicine chalets for seventy-five cents, visited nearby Trick Falls, then returned to Glacier Park Hotel in time for dinner. It was an inexpensive mini-vacation that the railway hoped would lure people to return.

For those staying longer, saddle horse trips were the big attraction at Two Medicine Chalets, ranging from half-day jaunts to the Inside Trail tour that lasted up to five days. A popular ride was to Mount Henry for the opportunity to ring a railway bell, one of four the Great Northern had installed at passes throughout Glacier (the others were at Swiftcurrent, Piegan and Siyeh). Ringing the bell mimicked a Swiss tradition and annoyed Park Service personnel, who had authorized a single bell, as a test, and worried that the clanging upset wildlife. The bells remained in service until 1943 when they were removed during a war scrap-metal drive.

"Scenery is a hollow enjoyment if the tourist starts out after an indigestible breakfast and a fitful sleep on an impossible bed," wrote Stephen Mather, head of the National Park Service. Chalet managers worked diligently to ensure guests were provided hearty, wholesome meals. Waitresses were responsible for the "fresh appearance" of their tables and were expected to arrange fresh flowers daily in the blue and brown bean pots. Personal cleanliness and neatness were emphasized, with waitresses instructed to arrange their hair so it would not have to be touched while they were on duty.

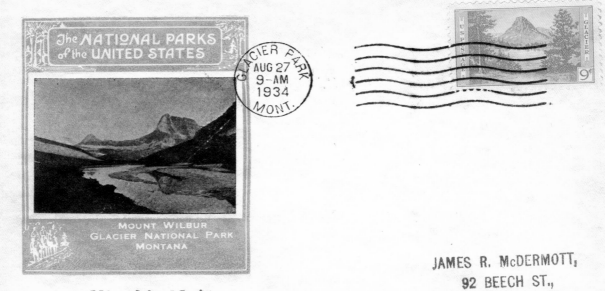

More than 52,000 Glacier Park stamps, featuring Mount Sinopah at Two Medicine Lake, were sold to collectors nationwide on their first day of issue. Ten clerks from five Montana cities came to Glacier to handle the orders, which bore park cancellations. During the first week, as piles of requests mailed from all over the world poured into the Glacier Park post office, postmistress Mrs. Harry M. Ralston seconded a room at Mike's Place to handle the extra business. This was the fifth stamp issued in a set of ten honoring national parks, and the first to recognize a Montana location.

The bell on Mount Henry sounded more than the arrival of riders; its installation in 1929 might well have been ringing in a new era: the Great Depression. Railway officials, like many other businessmen, were uncertain how long the economic downturn would last and in 1930, at least, operated on the principle they should maintain business as usual.

Visits by celebrities and VIPs were always good for generating news and thereby boosting business, so when the Great Northern learned President Herbert Hoover was being invited to Montana that summer to fly fish, his favorite pastime, the hotel company began making preparations at Two Medicine to welcome the president. The company built a new telephone line from the lake to the Glacier Park Station, and remodeled the chalets for inside plumbing and bathrooms. The work cost more than $16,500, but the Great Northern hoped the investment would be repaid by the publicity. Two Medicine was chosen not only for its fishing opportunities, but also because its single-road access and relative isolation provided the security and sanctuary necessary for a visiting president. Unfortunately, Hoover had to cancel the trip when business interceded.

The sting of the unfulfilled expense was more than soothed in 1934 when President Franklin Delano Roosevelt came to Glacier Park. Accompanied by his wife Eleanor and their three sons, Franklin Jr., John, and James, FDR arrived at Belton Station on August 5, 1934, and was chauffeured over newly opened Going-to-the-Sun Highway, ending up at Two Medicine Chalets, which had been vacated for the president.

Hundreds of people gathered at Two Medicine to watch thirty Blackfeet dance in traditional dress, make Roosevelt an honorary tribal member, and present him with a feathered headdress and the title Lone Chief. Eleanor was named Medicine Pipe Woman. All the while, Roosevelt never left the seat of his touring car. "I was taken completely by surprise when the Secret Service men lifted him out of the limousine, adjusted his braces and placed him in a wheelchair," said Canadian bandleader Mart Kenney, who happened to be in the park that day. "Like many people, I was not aware of the president's disability." A ramp was built at the chalets specifically to accommodate FDR's wheelchair.

With the formalities over, Eleanor and her sons took a quick dip in the chilly lake before sitting down to a private family dinner in one of the chalets. At 7:30 p.m. Roosevelt addressed the nation by radio from the dining hall at Two Medicine. Contrary to later reports, the broadcast was not an official "fireside chat," of which Roosevelt gave only two in 1934. Although the Roosevelts had been scheduled to stay the night, plans were changed, and they left for Glacier Park Station, sleeping aboard the presidential train and leaving early the next morning.

Roosevelt's trip did wonders for tourism to Glacier, boosting visitation generally and making Two Medicine Chalets one of the most requested stops in the park.

Two Medicine got another shot of publicity three years later, in September 1937, when J. Edgar Hoover, head of the Federal Bureau of

The Great Northern's hotel company paid $194 each for four locomotive bells it installed at passes throughout Glacier Park in the 1920s. The National Park Service was reluctant to grant permission until park service director Stephen Mather personally intervened. Installation of a single bell was approved as a test. Long before permission arrived, though, the railway had installed all the bells, permanently. The bells provided hikers and riders with a way to signal they'd reached the summits.

Investigation, stayed at the chalets. Like Roosevelt, Hoover was made an honorary Blackfeet and given the name Chief Eagle.

Such high profile guests made Two Medicine a must-see site, but did not keep chalet rooms filled with paying guests or help the hotel company recover from what became chronic annual losses in the 1930s. Despite National Park Service pressure to renovate the chalets, the railway refused. It also rejected a study it had commissioned that recommended replacing the chalets with six circles of cabins, similar to Swiftcurrent auto camp at Many Glacier. Instead, the hotel company cut its staffing and losses by reducing guest capacity to seventy, down from a 1927 high of 118.

During World War II, the United States Army Air Force proposed leasing the chalets as a rest and recreation center for air crews, later proposing to use the chalets, along with Glacier Park Hotel, as sites for arctic training. The plans never came off.

When Two Medicine Chalets reopened on June 15, 1946, the house count dropped even further, to fifty-eight, as rooms were taken out of service because they were falling into disrepair. The post-war boom and a huge increase in travel to Glacier failed to revive business at the chalets. Two Medicine remained as a sightseeing stop on bus tours, but handled few overnight guests, especially with the demise of the Park Saddle Horse Company.

In 1952, the Park Service approached the hotel company about tearing down Two Medicine Chalets due to their potential as fire hazards, leaving just the main dining hall to operate as a store for travelers using the nearby government campground. Great Northern president John Budd reluctantly agreed.

"Believe me, the decision to close Two Medicine was not made easily," Budd wrote later. "I have spent a great deal of time in my life in Glacier Park, particularly on its trails and knew some of the territory well. The problems we have faced in the park are heart-breaking under the circumstances."

When John Mauff of Chicago, an annual park visitor, learned of the plan to raze the chalets, he started a one-man letter writing campaign to save them. Unable to stop the demolition, Mauff did win a small coup. For a couple of years Budd gave him permission to be the chalet's sole guest, staying with manager Carl Karnes and his wife, Jo. "John Budd…realized what the end of the chalets meant to me, and

In the 1950s, Carl and Jo Karnes ran the "camp store" at Two Medicine, the sole remaining building from the chalet group after the rest were burned down in May 1956. The couple sold groceries, meats, fruits, vegetables, souvenirs, tobacco, candy, soft drinks, beer and camera film. Photo developing and finishing work was accepted, and fishing tackle rented and sold. No regular meals and lodging were available.

COURTESY OF MINNESOTA HISTORICAL SOCIETY

did what he could in his role…to enable at least one person to continue to enjoy and cherish [them]," said Mauff.

Demolition started in September 1955, ending in May 1956 when the last cabins were burned down; Wesley House of Browning, Montana, was contracted to do the job. Only the dining hall turned camp store was left standing.

In December 1960, the Great Northern sold the dining hall to Glacier Park Inc. of Tucson, Arizona. It was sold again in 1981 when Glacier Park Inc. was bought by what is now Viad Corp.

In 1987 the two-story log Two Medicine Store was designated a National Historic Landmark. The building remains relatively unchanged from when it was built. It is one of only three remaining examples of log construction used by the Great Northern for its chalets in Glacier Park—a last proud reminder of the chalet group that once stood at the foot of Two Medicine Lake.

Responding to increased demand, in 1926 the park service announced plans to improve the campground at Two Medicine Lake, a half mile from the chalets. Thirty sites were built, with tables and open fireplaces for cooking. Camping grew in popularity during the 1920s as cars became more affordable and reliable, allowing families to take extended outings.

Located on the south bank of the Cut Bank Creek in the shadow of Twin Buttes, Cut Bank Chalets were the halfway point for saddle horse trips between Two Medicine Lake and St. Mary Lake. Only four buildings comprised the chalet colony and for a time they were a popular rendezvous for fishermen. The footbridge behind the dining hall gave anglers easy access to the other side of the creek. In 1915, bus fare for a round trip to Cut Bank from Midvale was $4.50.

— Chapter 4 —
Cut Bank Chalets

The ability of man to outwit a fish and how far he will travel to do so is at the heart of the short life and renown of Cut Bank Chalets. For decades, sport fishermen flocked to this isolated and verdant valley of Glacier National Park to stay at the chalets and cast flies and lures into the nearby "singing mountain streams" in search of the elusive "big one"—cutthroat, eastern, and rainbow trout that weigh five pounds and up.

Cut Bank is a densely wooded valley of pines and firs six miles off the beaten path of the Blackfeet Highway. Then as now, the Cut Bank Valley is a tourism backwater. Even in earlier times it was little visited, although Cut Bank Pass was well known to the people of the Salish and Kootenai tribes. They had once dwelled on the prairies in the shadow of the Rockies, but were forced off the plains by the fearsome and better-armed Blackfeet. After fleeing across the mountains, the Salish and Kootenai made pilgrimages to the prairies to hunt bison and other game. Cut Bank Pass was one of their routes.

White men, explorers and otherwise, were also familiar with, but infrequent users of, Cut Bank Pass. Among those known or believed to have been over it are: Father Pierre DeSmet, the famed Jesuit priest, in 1845; Lt. A.W. Tinkham in 1853; Lt. Charles A. Woodruff and Lt. John T. Van Orsdale in 1873; and Prof. Raphael Pumpelly in 1883. Pumpelly marveled at the beauty of the region: "Among these limestone mountains—from lofty crest and in cirques—you will see the grandest scenery in the United States."

Louis Hill certainly agreed.

Even before the Cut Bank Chalets were opened for business in 1913, Great Northern had a teepee camp set up nearby. The teepees were a canvas imitation of those used by the Blackfeet. Each contained two cots, a wash stand, chairs, and kerosene or candle lamp. At fifty cents a night for a bed, the camps were economical for hikers and horse riders.

Joseph Scheuerle did many illustrations like this for the Great Northern's advertising and publicity department.

The stark contrast of luxurious service in primitive conditions at Cut Bank Chalets is evident in this image from a stereograph taken by N.A. Forsyth of Butte, Montana, about 1912. The folding chair is next to a table with two-by-four legs, the rough top of which is hidden under a linen table cloth. The waitress, in her dark grey uniform with starched white apron, inspects the setting. This view is one of thirty-one that Forsyth took on an expedition to Glacier, and sold as a set or individually.

Construction of Cut Bank Chalets began in late 1911 or early 1912. By the fall of 1913 the complex consisted of: an 18-by-80-foot dining room/kitchen building; two 18-foot-square, one-room cabins; and a two-story, 28-foot-square, six-room cabin with lounging area. They could handle forty-two guests.

At the time, no hiking or riding trail connected Two Medicine and Cut Bank. Guests instead had to take the stagecoach, car or bus to the chalets. A trail would not be built until 1915.

The facilities were definitely "rustic," to use a favorite railway euphemism. Guests made do with outhouses or, at night, chamber pots. There is contradictory evidence about whether rooms had running water. If there was running water, it would have been cold only. Initially, candles or kerosene lamps provided lighting. Later, a gas-fired power plant was installed. The rooms had no telephones, but guests could reach the outside world from the main desk, where the manager daily called the hotel company's headquarters, indicating the number of guests and supply requirements. By 1924 telegraph communication to other points in the park was possible. Laundry went out daily on a truck that delivered fresh linen and supplies.

The chalets' most formal place was the dining room. Guests were not expected to dress for dinner. "None of the staid conventions that take the edge off of sport follow you to this land of winding trails," a railway brochure notified potential visitors. "You can be yourself 24 hours a day, forgetful of care, extravagant with your energy, here today and there tomorrow."

Cut Bank Chalets were a stop on the Inside Trail saddle horse tour. The original three-day tour started at Glacier Park Hotel, ended at St. Mary Chalets, and cost $13.25, all expenses included. The five-day variation, from Glacier Park Hotel to Many Glacier, was $18.

Trail rides were popular with eastern tourists wanting to experience the Wild West. Great Northern copywriters went to great lengths to assure the timid they had nothing to fear taking unknown horses across 7,600-foot-high Pitamakan Pass. "Western horses are sure-footed and gentle....Even if you haven't been on a horse before it's a fine experience—and lots of fun." Early literature also reminded gentlefolk that "all riding is western style—astride the saddle."

The job of guaranteeing dudes' comfort went to wranglers of the Bar X6 Ranch, home base for the Park Saddle Horse Company. Tall tales were the order of the day, whether told in the saddle to pass the time, or around a campfire at lunch or after dinner.

"Speaking of sheep, we have the usual bighorn," wrangler Jim Whilt wrote in a compilation of fibs entitled *Giggles from Glacier Guides*, published in the 1930s. "Some old rams have horns so large they are unable to carry them naturally. They have conceived the idea of putting two small wheels under their chins so as to support the weight of their horns. In the winter they substitute runners in place of wheels."

For riders heading north on the Inside Trail, the goal was to reach Red Eagle Lake. If fishermen thought the angling at Cut Bank was great, Red Eagle was said to be spectacular. Initially it was a rest stop on the twenty-three-mile ride to St. Mary Chalets; there were no accommodations. Anyone who wanted to fish for more than an hour or two had to make a return trip from St. Mary Chalets.

Red Eagle Lake was so popular as a side trip that the Great Northern considered constructing a chalet colony at the site. It proposed a sleeping building, dining room, and laundry. Chief engineer Albert Hogeland said the trail needed improvements in only two or three places to make it good for wagons. Neither the road nor the buildings were built.

A tent camp at Red Eagle Lake opened in 1926. "[Riders] were met with great hospitality, given a cold drink on a hot day and a warm drink on a cold day," said Edwina Noffsinger, wife of Park Saddle Horse Company owner George Noffsinger and daughter-in-law of the founder. "A camp boy had pitchers of hot water for them in their tent houses…with good beds and beautiful Pendleton blankets on the beds and white sheets."

Business flourished at Red Eagle Lake camp and Cut Bank Chalets during the 1920s, with fishermen bolstering the ranks of dudes looking for mountain vacations and escaping hot summers in east-

Above: *A fine day's catch in the mountains, as set up for a Great Northern publicity picture. The railway often sponsored newspaper and magazine writers on paid vacations to the park.*

Below: *Red Eagle Lake tent camp, created in 1926, was a popular stop on the Inside Trail riding tour, operated by the Park Saddle Horse Company. Wranglers working for the Bar X6 Ranch, home base of the Park Saddle Horse Company, liked to joke the fish were so large in Red Eagle that it could take a day or more for the lake to return to normal level after a lunker was pulled out.*

Left: *Saddle horse guides were responsible not only for the well-being of their human charges, but also that of their mounts and the packhorses. Here, a wrangler shows his prowess at tying a load on a pack animal. The diamond hitch was the favored method of securing goods, but not the only one. Every wrangler seemed to have his own tying style and knots.*

Below: *Tent flaps have been lifted to air out accommodations for Park Saddle Horse Company wranglers. While the photo was taken at Kintla Lake, it is reflective of all Park Saddle Horse Company tent camps. "You ask: What is a tent camp?" a Great Northern brochure stated, "Let me tell you….Here you eat meals that would do credit to an urban hotel although every pound of foodstuffs must be packed in on horseback. You sleep in tents with painted board floors and side wall, and wood-burning heaters. The beds are good and blankets plentiful. After dinner the host lights the big fire and he and the guides regale their guests with true stories of the mountains and mountain men. Who cares if the true stories swell with imagined details? For a dash of imagination only adds to the thrills."*

ern cities. It was sufficiently brisk that the Great Northern felt confident enough in a 1924 brochure to eschew the trend toward park visitors arriving by automobile. "The Cut Bank Chalets are not of much interest to those traveling by auto, but my how good they look to the hiker or horse rider." The "intensely scenic" area is appreciated "only by those taking the Inside Trail trip." It was gratuitous advice that would hurt the railway six years later.

When the Depression hit and few people could afford to take saddle horse trips, the railway found it nearly impossible to lure visitors to Cut Bank. It was of little help that Glacier Park Transport Company had quit providing regular bus service. The railway, in conjunction with the Park Saddle Horse Company, tried luring people on trail rides by cutting prices. The incentives failed to stem the loss of visitors.

Use of Cut Bank Chalets fell so low that the railway did not open them for summer 1933. They remained boarded up until the summer of 1937. To prevent tourists' showing up, the Great Northern removed the name Cut Bank from maps in its brochures, although the National Park Service continued to list it.

The chalets' closure cut a stop on Noffsinger's Inside Trail ride, effectively ending it for the period. In 1937 Noffsinger suggested turning Cut Bank Chalets into a dude ranch. The Great Northern encouraged the experiment in the hope Noffsinger would take them over. The arrange-

The porch and upstairs balcony of this two-story chalet at Cut Bank provided many hours of relaxation for guests. Each summer, staff had to help with maintenance by removing shutters, cleaning up after pack rats that seemed to infest the camp over winter, freshening rooms, staining weather-worn woodwork and, at times, replacing chinking between the logs.

Going over 7,600-foot-high "Cut Bank Pass" was listed as one of the highlights of the ride between Two Medicine and Cut Bank chalets. The pass was in fact incorrectly listed for decades in railway brochures, and correctly is Pitamakan Pass. Cut Bank Pass is nearby and higher, traversing the Continental Divide and leading to the Nyack Valley. It took years to revise maps to correct the confusion, which nonetheless persists.

ment was deemed a failure, however, because Noffsinger could not convince the hotel company to forgo a cut of the take.

The hotel company could no longer justify maintaining the chalets, and requested permission from the park superintendent to close them in 1938. They were never reopened.

Red Eagle Lake camp stayed open during the Depression, but fishing trips no longer emanated from St. Mary Chalets, which also closed for lack of business. Instead, trips to Red Eagle Lake were offered from Going-to-the-Sun Chalets, and were listed as a two-day package to account for the greater distance.

When the Great Northern reopened its facilities after World War II, Cut Bank Chalets were regarded as beyond repair. During the winter of 1948-1949 a railway crew, under the direction of contractor Fred Stone, began dismantling the site. What couldn't be salvaged was burned.

Today, the Cut Bank Valley has returned to the peace and quiet it once knew. Glacier officials desire to maintain the area's tranquillity, designating it a "rustic zone" primarily for day use. The road into Cut Bank is still gravel. That does not deter fishermen, however, who continue to flock to this corner of the park and trade stories about the huge fighting trout that inhabit Cut Bank Creek.

Good chalet managers were important to customer service at remote sites such as Cut Bank, above. In 1925, T.E. Rhoads and his wife shared the duties at Cut Bank. The forty-five-year-old Rhoads, though older than many chalet managers, acquitted himself well during his tenure, having learned the hotel business in Perry, Iowa, where he had cooked for twelve years and operated a sixty-room hotel. He was typical of the people Glacier Park Hotel Company sought as chalet managers: former hotel and boarding house staff—and school teachers, who were prized because they could work the summer, were well versed in people-handling skills and well educated.

A Glacier Park Transportation Company bus loaded with tourists waits briefly outside the main dining hall at St. Mary Chalets in the 1920s. Although touted as a destination resort, the chalets saw most tourists pass through quickly when regular bus service started in 1915, headed for Going-to-the-Sun Chalets or Many Glacier Hotel. The dining hall at St. Mary also served as the complex's lobby, and was where the transportation agent answered queries and helped guests plan itineraries. On the right, the dining room windows overlook the lake. The hotel company removed any trees that obstructed the view.

— Chapter 5 —
St. Mary Chalets

If there was ever a hotel site in Glacier Park that was under-appreciated and under-used by the Great Northern Railway, it was that of St. Mary Chalets. For much of their life St. Mary Chalets were a glorified transit station—a brief stop for visitors on the way to somewhere else, whether by bus, boat, or horseback, or on foot. Although advertised as a destination resort, the chalets could not compete with attractions at other locations. St. Mary Chalets were a popular "going in" point, easy to get to but also just as easy to leave. Ultimately, that helped lead to their demise.

St. Mary Chalets were built on a ten-acre site at the foot of ten-mile-long St. Mary Lake. They were situated in a grove of pines and deciduous trees, and constructed into the side of a hill, facing west. "You forget every lake you have ever seen before in all your life," author Agnes C. Laut said of St. Mary Lake.

The chalets were preceded by a teepee camp during the 1911 season while construction of cabins began. Nine major buildings would be built over a period of three years. The first structures were four cabins and a cookhouse. The Great Northern used a cookie-cutter pattern for the cabins so those at Two Medicine and Cut Bank were identical to those at St. Mary. Over the next two years, the railway would complete the colony. Added were a 42-by-85-foot dining room and kitchen to replace the earlier one, a "recreation building," a two-story guest dormitory that measured 28 by 84 feet, and several outbuildings. In total, the complex could sleep 150 guests.

The Great Northern advertised St. Mary Chalets as "attractive rustic buildings, and no attempt is made to provide unnecessary service. The beds are comfortable, and three plain, wholesome meals a day are provided, served in family style." The location was the start of "many pleasant walks." Fishermen were advised that "it is eight miles from St. Mary to Red Eagle Lake, the home of the cutthroat trout."

All baggage in transit was designated with a tag that would later double as a visitor's souvenir. Louis Hill directed all hotels and camps be furnished with a supply so they would be applied "daily to all baggage possible." Great Northern also issued a series of postage-style stamps, one or more for each chalet and hotel, in the mid-1910s as a novel way to promote travel to Glacier Park. Tens of thousands were printed.

Right: The main dining hall at St. Mary Chalets was a hub of activity with the twice daily arrival and departure of tour buses and boats. Here, gear-jammers await their charges.

Below: The launch St. Mary rests at dock. Built by Captain William Swanson, the boat carried passengers between St. Mary and Going-to-the-Sun chalets until the 1940s. In 1951 it was sold to Barney Rankin for use on Flathead Lake. A fire in 1960 destroyed the vessel.

3111 BUSSES AT ST. MARYS CHALETS, GLACIER NATIONAL PARK

The lure of the St. Mary lakes was more than just the result of lavish prose heaped on the area by Great Northern's copy writers. Americans had been reading about them long before in the articles James Willard Schultz submitted regularly to *Forest and Stream* magazine. Schultz was a curiosity, a "white Blackfeet." He came west to Fort Benton, Montana, in 1877, quickly fell into a native lifestyle, marrying a Peigan girl, and "participating fully in all of the Indian modes of life."

Schultz's stories about the Blackfeet were more than just romantic tales. He documented their plight, how they lived in poverty on the reservation, how their traditional way of life had been taken with the slaughter of the buffalo, and how their population had been decimated by epidemics. The articles were so compelling they prompted the magazine's editor and publisher, George Bird Grinnell, to visit Glacier for himself.

G114. St. Marys Chalets and Lake St. Marys, Glacier National Park

Grinnell became a major player in the region. He christened many of the local mountains, visited a glacier that now bears his name, participated as a federal commissioner in the negotiations that persuaded the Blackfeet to sell the mountainous area of their reservation in 1896—land that would become a major part of Glacier Park—and was the most prominent and vocal lobbyist for the establishment of Glacier National Park.

The St. Mary Chalets opened on June 15, 1913. Guests arrived by stagecoach or chauffeured car, both services provided by the Brewster brothers. The thirty-six-mile trip from Midvale took 2½ hours by car, or half a day by stagecoach, including the stop at Cut Bank Chalets.

For stagecoach riders, St. Mary Chalets was an overnight stay before catching a boat to Going-to-the-Sun Chalets or continuing by road to Many Glacier Camp. The stagecoaches proved unreliable and the Great Northern eventually dropped the Brewsters in favor of the Glacier Park Transportation Company's red buses.

Regular bus service changed the nature of St. Mary Chalets. Visitors often came and went the same day, staying only for a short rest and lunch. Great Northern brochures noted that "for a period of an hour in the morning and another in the afternoon, when the buses and boat arrive and depart, St. Mary is the scene of much activity, but ordinarily it is a quiet and restful place, attractive as an economical stopping place for trail riders and fishermen."

Even riders ending the Inside Trail saddle horse trip did not linger, being offered three exit routes: Sun Camp, Many Glacier Chalets, and back to Midvale where the tour originated.

With the bulk of visitors whisked through, St. Mary Chalets came to rely on tourists using private automobiles. In those days, the Blackfeet Highway ran right by the chalets. The recreation hall at St. Mary Chalets served as a supply store for campers, and refreshment stand for those who didn't want a meal in the dining room.

The auto-tourist business did not last, however. It was undermined starting in 1926 when Montana began rebuilding the Blackfeet Highway. The road was realigned, bypassing the chalets, now reached only by a spur off the highway. Linked to rebuilding the Blackfeet Highway was the beginning of construction on Going-to-the-Sun Highway. The two roads intersected at "Old Town," an unincorporated summer village that was revitalized by the construction, and eventually took the name of St. Mary. Restaurants, motels, and gas stations sprang up in St. Mary to serve travelers. Business owners liked the junction's location just outside

The creation of Glacier National Park owes much to naturalist George Bird Grinnell (1849-1938), who published many articles about the area and wrote extensively of his own visits. It's ironic that, despite his name's being so prominent in the park, it was unrecognized by a Many Glacier Hotel clerk in the 1920s when the notable guest registered there.

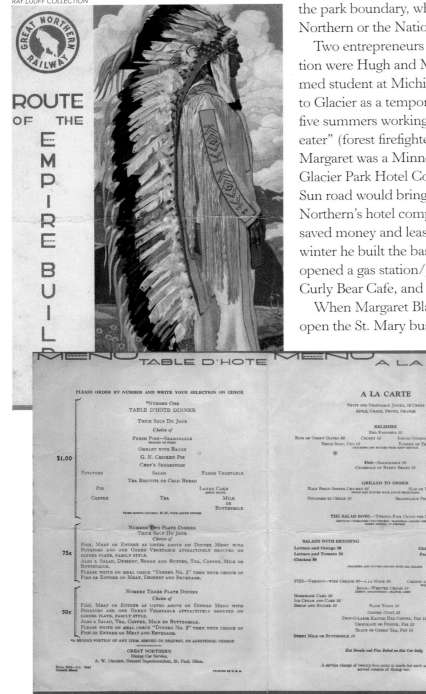

the park boundary, where they were not subject to the Great Northern or the National Park Service.

Two entrepreneurs who staked their future on St. Mary junction were Hugh and Margaret Black. Hugh Black was a pre-med student at Michigan State College in 1926 when he came to Glacier as a temporary summer ranger. He returned the next five summers working in various roles, from ranger to "smoke eater" (forest firefighter), all the while growing to love the park. Margaret was a Minnesotan who worked year-round for the Glacier Park Hotel Company. Hugh Black felt Going-to-the-Sun road would bring thousands more tourists than Great Northern's hotel company could handle. He and Margaret saved money and leased land at St. Mary junction. Over one winter he built the basis for the family enterprise, and in 1932 opened a gas station/general store, a restaurant called the Curly Bear Cafe, and six small rental cabins.

When Margaret Black left her job with the hotel company to open the St. Mary business, she said her Great Northern bosses didn't think it would amount to anything. The facilities were rustic, but the self-assured Blacks pressed on, using humor and honesty to build their business. "When customers asked if the cabins had running water, Hugh would say: 'Yes, look at the stream that runs by your front door. Modern? Why we just built them last week.'" With the initial success of the gas station and rental cabins, Hugh constructed a bigger restaurant, the St. Mary Cafe, in 1938, and added more cabins and a motel.

Painter Winold Reiss's portraits of Blackfeet natives were used extensively by the Great Northern to promote travel to Glacier, such as on this Empire Builder dining car menu.

The St. Mary Cafe quickly established a reputation for excellent, affordable food, thanks in no small part to the cook, Ralph Plunkett. Margaret Black said hiring Plunkett was a fortuitous accident. "We were so lucky....Ralph Plunkett thought he was coming to a big hotel. He had worked in New York and came west for his health," she said. Plunkett was taken aback when he saw the tiny diner where he'd signed on, but stuck it out and remained with the Blacks until World War II. "Our shanghaied cook he used to call himself," Margaret said. "He was wonderful. He built up our reputation; we owe him a lot."

The Great Northern had plans of its own for a motel at St. Mary junction, but Louis Hill wanted to wait until Going-to-the-Sun road was completed to see what impact it would have on business at St. Mary Chalets. When the road opened in July 1933, entrepreneurs at St. Mary junction profited from the jump in visitation, not the chalets. Hill's plan for "auto cabins" never materialized. He had stepped down as chairman of the railway four years earlier and, with the onset of the Depression, motel plans were put on the back burner.

Set out of sight from the highway, St. Mary Chalets went nearly unnoticed by motorists hurrying over Going-to-the-Sun road. Hollywood actor Clark Gable was one of those motorists. He stopped at a store at St. Mary junction only long enough to buy a bottle of Coke. Local kids made a tidy profit selling a case of empties to tourists saying each was the bottle Gable drank from.

With too few customers, St. Mary Chalets were not opened to the public during the 1934 season, but launch service between the chalets and Sun Camp continued to operate with the support of the daily bus arrivals.

The chalets were temporarily saved from closure by happenstance. Winold Reiss was looking for a location to set up a summer art school in the park. The artist taught mural painting at the College of Fine Arts of New York University. Reiss had a fascination with painting Native Americans, particularly the Blackfeet, and the railway was always looking for artists whose work it used for advertising and promotion.

"I think this man is one of the best prospects we have had in the way of artists painting Indian pictures, which are our strongest feature," Hill said after seeing Reiss's work for the first time. Commissions in 1927 and 1928 proved Hill right. The railroad bought every portrait Reiss produced, using them as the basis for the railway's first Indian calendar.

"As near as I can find out from all our outside men, this calendar is considered very high class publicity for our line....So far as the Indian calendars are concerned, no one can do them the justice as can Winold Reiss," said railway vice-president William Kenney. The railway would continue issuing calendars with Reiss's paintings for thirty years.

So when Reiss proposed the idea of holding a summer school in Glacier, railway officials were attentive. Placing the school in St. Mary Chalets, near the reservation where Reiss found his models, would earn

Hollywood film star Clark Gable made his first visit to Glacier Park in July 1937 before retreating to the Charles Jennings ranch, fourteen miles southwest of the park, to hunt bears. Blackfeet natives Middle Calf, left, and Theodore Last Star treated Gable to a "good-hunting ceremony." Gable's stay that trip was cut short by a call from his film production company in California, but Gable became a frequent visitor over the next few years.

the hotel company a modest income, and keep the buildings in use.

The St. Mary art school ran four summers (1934-1937) under the auspices of New York's College of Fine Arts. Students paid $70 for a two-month course or $90 for three months. Room and board was $240 and $300 respectively. The majority of attendees were Reiss's students from New York, although the school did draw participants from as far afield as Fitchburg, Massachusetts, Holly, Colorado, and Monroe, Washington. Staff included Reiss, his brother, Hans, a sculptor and sometime climbing guide for the Park Saddle Horse Company, and Carl Link, Reiss's friend and a portrait and landscape artist.

The art school offered instruction in sculpture and drawing. "The students who desire to paint landscapes will find beautiful scenery all around the camp," an art school brochure claimed, although few students exercised that option. Rather, they wanted to use the same Blackfeet models who posed for Reiss. For while Reiss ran the art school, he also had a commitment to the Great Northern to produce new images for railroad calendars.

"Winold was a very good teacher," recalled student Karola Miener (nee Mankenberg). "Winold always found something nice to say about your picture, and then with a slight touch of a finger rubbing out or adding a line, your picture was OK. He also insisted that parts were done again, but seemed to know how far or how much to criticize each picture according to the pupil."

Winold Reiss, **top**, had such a fascination with North American natives he emigrated from Germany to America in 1913 so he could learn more about them and paint them. Reiss's brother, Hans, a climbing guide at Many Glacier Hotel, introduced Winold to Louis Hill. For four summers Reiss and Hans ran an art school at St. Mary Chalets. **Above**, a student sculpts a bust of a Blackfeet native on the porch of the recreation hall.

The art school attracted many visitors and helped launch the careers of several artists. English sculptor, journalist, and author Clare Sheridan spent the summer of 1937 at the school to sculpt. During a visit to the Blood reserve, Sheridan spotted potential talent in eleven-year-old Gerald Tailfeathers. Reiss offered him free instruction, and Tailfeathers became a noted painter and sculptor. Two other successful native students were Albert Racine and Victor Pepion. Elizabeth Davey Lochrie, a mature student, later worked as a staff artist for the Great Northern.

The art school was less successful at generating revenue, never drawing as many students as Reiss or railway officials hoped. By 1937, both concluded the school was more trouble than it was worth, and that was its last year.

Although there was an upswing in tourism to Glacier prior to World War II, the St. Mary Chalets were ignored by both the public and the railway. Neither government nor Great Northern brochures listed them, and they weren't included on bus routes. Adolph Aszmann, hotel company manager, advised the Park Service: "When the Roes Creek [Rising Sun] cabin facilities have been completed and are ready to operate, I really see no reason why St. Mary Chalets should be kept open." The chalets were never reopened.

During the war, the chalets were considered as a site for arctic survival training for the military, but the project was never approved. In 1943, the Great Northern announced that the St. Mary buildings would be dismantled, except for the boathouse and dock for the boat *St. Mary*. Ironically, Hugh Black won the bid to remove them.

Today, the only reminders of St. Mary Chalets are a few buildings' concrete foundations and the dock's wooden piers. The site is unmarked, and few people search it out. Those who come across it, about a mile south of the St. Mary Visitor Center, do so accidentally and are usually puzzled. It is an ignoble end for a chalet colony, but perhaps not unfitting: As it was overlooked when it existed, so it continues today.

A pair of sunbathers make use of the dock and a Great Northern blanket at St. Mary Chalets (the guest dormitory is visible in the upper right). Students at Winold Reiss's art school would often use the boat dock for their afternoon break, many times dragging along a gramophone. Swimming is possible in the glacier- and mountain-stream–fed lake, but only advised for those with strong constitutions.

—Chapter 6—

Going-to-the-Sun Chalets

G oing-to-the-Sun Chalets lasted only thirty years before they fell victim to progress, yet in that time they were the most popular chalets in the park.

Perched about 100 feet atop a windswept outcrop at the narrows of St. Mary Lake below Goat Mountain, this small alpine village was the ultimate chalet group. Sun Camp, as it was sometimes called, was the largest of the chalet colonies in Great Northern's system, and its services and features rivaled those of the "bigger" hotels. It provided accommodations as comfortable, one of the greatest views in America, invigorating contact with nature, and the widest variety of trips.

The facilities started very much like those at other locations. A temporary camp, reached by saddle horse, was established in 1911 on a two-acre plot along Baring Creek.

The site for the permanent buildings was about a quarter of a mile away. Logs were cut at the upper end of St. Mary Lake, floated down, then lifted up the cliff face to the construction site. By 1912 work crews had completed a kitchen/dining room, five one-room cabins, and a two-story log building complete with lounging rooms on both levels. The facilities could handle thirty-eight guests.

Due to its location, and the absence of a road, the railway provided boat transportation to the chalets. The *Red Eagle* and the *Glacier* were both thirty-two feet long, and carried twenty-five passengers each. The scenic fifty-five-minute ride from St. Mary Chalets helped put guests in the vacation spirit. As well, the boats carried luggage and supplies to the chalets. The chalets could also be reached by saddle horse or on foot. The first summer with permanent buildings, 1912, Sun Camp played host to 300 visitors.

With more buildings on the drawing board, and the planned opening of Glacier Park Hotel the next summer, the railway knew it would need a larger vessel. In 1913, the railway launched the 120-passenger, sixty-four-foot *St. Mary*, a sleek, comfortable boat with a fourteen-

For decades, Going-to-the-Sun Chalets were the most popular in Glacier because they served as a hub for a many trail rides and hikes. Going-to-the-Sun Highway (one of its tunnels is seen above) ultimately doomed the chalets. Until the road arrived, the chalets could be reached only by saddle horse or boat, an oasis of civilization in the wilderness, as exemplified by these nattily garbed guests outside the dining hall, (facing page). Above them and to the right are guest dormitories.

71

Overlooking St. Mary Lake, Going-to-the-Sun Chalets provided guests with spectacular views of both water and mountains, readily enjoyed from larger chalets **(above)** and one-room cabins **(below)**. On the spit of land opposite Sun Point, Louis Hill had two cabins built for his personal use, although he argued to the government they were for artists and guests who wanted the ultimate in privacy. Hill's remonstrations were undermined by the supply list for the cabins that had one fewer pillows than beds; presumably Hill brought his own. Hill's cabins were removed in 1944 by the Civilian Conservation Corps.

3003—GOING-TO-THE-SUN CHALETS, ST. MARYS LAKE, GLACIER NATIONAL PARK

foot beam that had been built by Captain William Swanson.

By 1915, under supervision of architect Thomas D. McMahon, an expansion of the Sun Camp complex was completed. It now included an enlarged dining room, laundry, and two spacious guest dormitory chalets that increased the sleeping capacity to 200 people, a figure that would vary over the years depending upon the arrangement of the beds. The comfort and resulting popularity of Sun Camp spoke for itself: some 2,814 overnight guests were accommodated in 1915, a figure that did not count numerous day visitors who arrived by boat only to enjoy lunch.

The camp offered relaxation in the wilderness—a mixture of formality and casualness. Here, as at other Great Northern facilities, linen-covered tables greeted hungry guests who were served by waitresses in Swiss costumes that lent a mountain theme. Hikers, especially, appreciated the all-you-could eat menu. Recalled one avid trekker who returned year after year: "I'll never forget how [the waitress] would bring in my super-substantial order, and stand by me with arms akimbo, and an expression of amazed disbelief, that I could 'manage' so much."

By day, Going-to-the Sun Chalets were where the action was. It was second only to the Many Glacier area as a center for guest activities, and became a hub for trail riders, hikers, and fishermen who found all the comforts of home, including the services of a resident nurse, telephone and telegraph communications, good meals, and the opportu-

Going-to-the-Sun Chalets were built precipitously on an outcrop of rock with balconies appearing to hang over open water, providing a great view of the approach of the launch St. Mary. During construction of Going-to-the-Sun Highway in the 1930s, tourists could watch as a barge plied the water taking supplies to the head of St. Mary Lake, where they would be unloaded for the building crew.

Cruising the calm waters of St. Mary Lake to mile high peaks

GOING-TO-THE-SUN CHALETS
St. Mary Lake, largest of the "east side" lakes, is a center
of rare Alpine beauty

AVERAGING less than a mile in width and about ten miles in length, St. Mary Lake presents an unusual landscape of rare charm. To the east and northeast stretch the rolling foothills of the Blackfeet Reserve, while to the west, hemming in the lake more and more as its upper limits are reached, are the serrated battlements of the Rockies culminating in the towers of Going-to-the-Sun.

At the lower end of the lake, thirty-four miles by auto road from the Glacier Park Hotel, are the St. Mary Chalets, facing westward across wind-swept waves to snow-crested peaks. This chalet group is the gateway to the St. Mary region of Glacier Park.

On St. Mary Lake launch service connects the St. Mary Chalets with the Going-to-the-Sun Chalets near the upper end of the lake, the trip taking approximately an hour.

The Going-to-the-Sun Chalet group is the largest of these groups in Glacier

Park. It is located on a high promontory at the base of Goat Mountain and from the chalet porches magnificent panoramas of lake and mountains stretch out on every side, while high above the snowfields of Going-to-the-Sun glisten in the sunlight.

For the hiker and horseman Going-to-the-Sun Chalets are second only to Many Glacier Hotel, for Sun Camp, as this place is commonly known, has been called the heart of Glacier Park. Every one of the longer scheduled tours can be made from this place. The Triangle Trip can be made via Many Glacier Hotel, Granite Park Chalets and return to Sun Camp via Logan Pass. The North Circle can also be taken from here by way of Logan Pass to Granite Park Chalets.

From Going-to-the-Sun Chalets a trail leads around the head of St. Mary Lake and up Red Eagle Creek to Red Eagle Lake, one of the best fishing lakes in the Park. The trip to the lake and return requires two days, but fisher-

The Going-to-the-Sun Chalets rise above the narrows of St. Mary Lake

This 1930s brochure touts the traditional way to see Glacier Park, via saddle horse tours.

nity to make new friends in the heart of the mountains. Row boats and fishing gear could be rented; then, as now, no fishing license was required within the park. The lakes in the Roes Creek basin, not far from the camp, offered the opportunity to catch mackinaw, while Gunsight Lake, nine miles away, offered rainbow trout.

Reconvening at Sun Camp, guests could gather around the lobby fireplace, and share their day's experiences, play board and card games, or study the ten Indian picture writings that adorned the walls. Going-to-the-Sun was the only chalet colony to display this kind of artwork.

Realizing that informed guests tended to stay longer, the hotel company encouraged presentations by park ranger-naturalists. In the 1920s and 1930s, Sun Camp was the only chalet grouping where these programs, under the direction of Dr. Morton Elrod, were routinely provided. In addition to a living flower display, rocks typical of park strata were exhibited, and the resident ranger-naturalist gave five- to twenty-five-minute talks in the lobby or, during lunch, in the dining room, as well as accompanying *St. Mary* voyages to explain the area's natural history.

While pleasant duty, it was also demanding both on and off the job, recalled Wilford Miller. He was a ranger-naturalist at Sun Camp for seven years under Elrod's successor, Dr. George Ruhle, the first permanent park naturalist. "Everything was geared to sharing the outdoors with others," said Miller, who credits his upbringing in rural North Dakota for his interest in, and respect for, nature and wildlife. Miller's knowledge of Glacier's flora, fauna, and geology impressed those who heard his lectures or joined him on a guided nature walk. "One person I remember clearly, said to me, 'I'd trade all my knowledge in law for your knowledge of nature.' I considered this a great compliment."

Sometimes nature itself came into the chalets, much to the chagrin of the hotel company that prided itself on clean, home-style accommodations. Pack rats, cute fluffy rodents that emit a vile smelling musk, were frequent intruders at Going-to-the-Sun Chalets. Every night they would appear in the lobby, running along the overhead beams, climbing down the pictures, and even getting into the dining room. These rambunctious rodents were even known to dismantle the carefully prepared living flower exhibits.

Sun Camp was the only chalet location where horses could be engaged for camping trips as well as for day trips. Guests who had never ridden were encouraged by wranglers to explore the back country, even if it meant giving them the basics of riding. With over 700 miles of trails in the park, more saddle horses—over 900—were used in Glacier than in any other park or recreational region in the country.

Guide Jim Whilt recalled inexperienced riders sometimes became confused over the difference between English and western style saddles. "One lady was asked which saddle she preferred, the English or western, and she asked what the difference was," Whilt said. "When told the western saddle had a horn, she said she would take the English saddle, as she thought the traffic would not be heavy enough for a horn."

Trails were of vital importance to Going-to-the-Sun Chalets' success as a resort and, when the Park Service was unable to maintain them, the railway would sometimes do so at its own expense. Louis Hill was constantly concerned about trail conditions, and did all he could to urge park officials to improve them.

United States entry into World War I pre-empted the hotel company's plan for a $9,460 improvement to Sun Camp. After the war, hotel company manager Howard Noble suggested a major expansion at Sun Point. Stephen Mather, head of the National Park Service, agreed, not-

Glacier Park naturalist George C. Ruhle, above, continued and expanded the interpretive work started by Dr. Morton Elrod. Ruhle's Guide to Glacier National Park, a spiral-bound book published in 1949, became required reading for every visitor. Ironically, Ruhle, who had worked in Glacier for the previous two decades, was posted at Crater Lake National Park when the book was released.

Construction of Going-to-the-Sun Highway, seen here against the backdrop of Mount Clements, went on for more than a decade, hobbled by limitations of the weather and government funding. The road has been designated a national historic landmark in recognition of its unique engineering, particularly the section carved out of the sheer cliffs of the Garden Wall.

ing in his 1920 annual report, "within the next year or two it will be necessary to convert the former chalet into a hotel" to accommodate 500 people. Ralph Budd, then railway president, saw the need as well. Hill rejected the idea, opting for smaller improvements, including construction of new rooms and a boat dock. Later, in 1926, a larger dining room and a lobby building were added, along with a sixty-room dormitory. The decision not to build the hotel at the site proved, in hindsight, to seal its future, one irrevocably tied to saddle horses.

Americans by the 1920s were becoming middle class urban residents. Automobiles extended the reach of those who could afford vacations, and also symbolized the modern, while horses meant old fashioned. The pressure to open the vast interior wilderness of Glacier to automobile traffic was enormous. In the mid-1920s, the long-time dream of many took off when construction began on Going-to-the-Sun Highway, a fifty-two-mile road traversing the Continental Divide at 6,664-foot Logan Pass. According to historian Warren Hanna, "the motivation for its construction was almost entirely to provide a means of viewing the park's great beauty for a few brief months each year, rather than to serve merely as a means of getting from one location to another." In essence, the new road supplanted the need to rent trail horses.

The road would take over a decade to finish and cost $3 million, more than the total Great Northern had spent on its hotels and chalets. Publicity about the scenic mountain route, opened in 1933, helped lure thousands to Glacier despite the Depression; the number of visitors jumped 43 percent to 76,000 in 1933 from 53,000 the previous year. It is estimated that 40,000 visitors drove the new road its first year.

Going-to-the-Sun Highway changed both Sun Camp's clientele and nature. It became a convenient place for tourists to stop for a meal,

refuel their vehicles, and glimpse the scenery, but not to stay for the night or begin a saddle horse trip. Less-expensive accommodations beckoned travelers, including a new free public campground at Roes Creek, a few miles east of Going-to-the-Sun Chalets, opened just in time for the new road.

Although Louis Hill toyed briefly with building a chalet at Logan Pass, he was unable to convince other executives of its value. By 1934 focus returned to improvements at Going-to-the-Sun Chalets, and the railway commissioned George H. Shanley, a Great Falls, Montana, architect, to draw preliminary plans for a building to replace many of the chalets and cabins. Those plans, too, fell by the wayside, due in large part to the depressed economy and falling railway passenger numbers.

In an effort to increase Great Northern passenger traffic stopping off

Snow removal on Going-to-the-Sun Road (its name since the 1950s) each spring is made dangerous by the avalanche risk. The start of work depends on weather, but usually begins in May. One day a year invited guests witness snow clearing on the only route directly linking the park's east and west sides. Motoring over Going-to-the-Sun Road is a one-of-a-kind driving experience.

in Glacier, the railway promoted the "new Logan Pass detour" as a side trip that included bus transportation over the road, meals, and accommodations at the Sun Camp. Many trips were sold, but not enough to rebuild room occupancy to what it was before Going-to-the Sun Highway. The Park Saddle Horse Company tried a similar campaign to boost trail rides—with equally disappointing results.

Great Northern officials were torn about what to do. Meanwhile, the Park Service requested that its concessioner, the reluctant railway, expand its facilities, particularly to build a motel—"auto cabins" as they were called at the time. The Great Northern didn't want to build auto cabins that would compete with existing chalets and hotels. At the same time, it was unwilling to invest in chalet upgrades, yet didn't want to abandon existing infrastructure.

Finally, after years of prodding, the hotel company announced it would build an auto camp at Roes Creek, the East Glacier Auto Cabins (now called Rising Sun Motor Inn.) The first eighteen cabins opened in 1940.

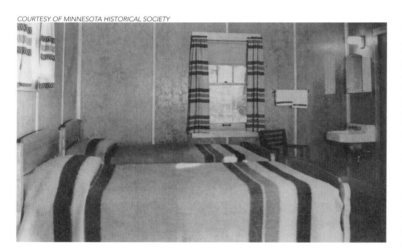

Rising Sun Auto Cabins, above, with their board-and-batten construction, provided inexpensive accommodations for tourists who traveled by private automobiles. Rooms were equipped with a sink, toilet, electric lights, heating stove, wood, table, chairs, bed, mattress and pillows. Meals were available at a nearby coffee shop, which featured a spacious lobby with a fireplace.

Each contained two non-connecting rooms, with cold running water, lavatory with or without a shower, electric lights, wood stove with a supply of wood, table, chairs, and two double beds. Two people renting a cabin without a shower paid $1.75. Linens were available at an extra charge. At the coffee shop, visitors could purchase three meals a day for a total of $1.30. By comparison, rooms at nearby Going-to-the-Sun Chalets ran from $4.50 to $7.50 per night, inclusive. The lobby adjoining the coffee shop had a fireplace and soda fountain. A camp store offered groceries, film, fishing tackle, and tobacco. Over the next two years, eighteen more units would be built.

The completion of fifty-two-mile-long Going-to the-Sun Highway changed the nature of tourism in Glacier Park. Sights such as Blackfoot Glacier, the largest in the park, could easily be seen from the road, so visitors no longer needed to and seldom took time for saddle horse trips.

Great Northern started using color photography, such as this image of waitresses at Going-to-the-Sun Chalets dining hall, to promote Glacier Park in the late 1930s.

Direct to the Vacation Gateway

GLACIER NATIONAL PARK
WATERTON LAKES PARK
NEARBY PARKS IN CANADIAN ROCKIES

GREAT NORTHERN RAILWAY

East Glacier Auto Cabins were the final blow to the aging Going-to-the-Sun Chalets. On August 1, 1941, park superintendent Donald S. Libby declared Sun Camp obsolete. "Under no conditions are minor modernizations recommended," he said, suggesting nothing less than a complete rebuilding would be acceptable. World War II intervened before plans could be implemented. By war's end, the buildings had fallen into disrepair, victims of the elements as much as neglect. In 1948 they were torn down, and the site restored to its natural state.

Today, there is little at Sun Point to remind tourists of the thriving and quaint chalet colony that once dominated activity in the interior of Glacier Park. Ironically, Going-to-the Sun Road and Rising Sun Motor Inn, both today identified as being of national historic significance, have survived but are threatened by old age and the need for costly repairs.

The lounge-dining room at "Sun Camp" was the hub around which a cluster of guest dormitory chalets were built. Railway brochures described it as having "log thatched ceilings, gay Indian blankets, potted pines, [a] huge fireplace" making the chalets as "picturesque within as they are without." Chefs could use their own recipes for dishes or rely on those from the railroad's dining car service, of which the Great Northern was exceptionally proud. It published a booklet called Great Northern Secrets, which featured its dining car chefs and recipes for such specialties as "Spaghetti a la Glacier Park," "Maitre d'Hotel Butter" and "Great Northern Baked Ham."

A focal point of the lobby of Many Glacier Hotel was the double helix staircase, which enclosed a stone fountain. Behind the staircase was the gift shop. The staircase led to The Grill, a combination soda fountain (prior to Prohibition's being lifted) and dance hall. Guests would complain when the revelers got too loud and the sound drifted up to the bedrooms surrounding the lobby. The design of Many Glacier Hotel exhibits elements of Adirondack "camp" style combined with Arts and Crafts motifs.

— Chapter 7 —
Many Glacier Hotel

A spire-topped walkway links the lobby of Many Glacier Hotel with the bedrooms in Annex 2, opened to guests in 1917. The spire was likely inspired by architect Kirtland Cutter's proposed design, which had just such a feature on the lobby portion. Louis Hill rejected Cutter's plan and had railway architect Thomas McMahon come up with new blueprints. When the porte cochere was added in the late 1950s, its design mimicked this spire.

When the magnificent, rambling, four-story Many Glacier Hotel opened to the public on July 4, 1915, Great Northern Railway was already promoting it as "one of the most noteworthy tourist hotels that ever has been erected in America."

"Many," as it was nicknamed, is fifty miles north from Glacier Park Station in the grandeur of Swiftcurrent Valley. The building cannot be said to face in any certain direction, since its three sections, totaling 600 feet in length, conform to the irregular shoreline of Swiftcurrent (then known as McDermott) Lake. At the north end are the kitchen and dining room, connected by the "long hall" in Annex 1 to the lobby, surrounded by tiers of guest rooms. Annex 2 was added in 1917.

The building was designed to harmonize with its setting and subtly improve on its older and by-then enlarged sister, Glacier Park Hotel. The forest-style lobby incorporated thirty-inch-diameter peeled log columns that rise four stories to the ceiling. It featured two fireplaces, one hooded and free-standing, around which guests could sit in the evenings to chat. At the south end was a one-of-a-kind double-helix staircase built around a cone-shaped fountain planted with native ferns and lit by colored lights.

A 180-foot mural canvas painted by Chief Medicine Owl and eleven other elders depicting the history of the Blackfeet tribe extended around the walls. The pictographs were so striking that two members of the American Rockies Alpine Club would later write it was "worth while to cross the continent to see…. It was painted expressly for the hotel and is unique among wall decorations."

Many Glacier offered guests the same high standard of amenities and service found at Glacier Park Hotel. It had a shoeshine stand, tailor and barber shops, infirmary, telephone and telegraph services, and transportation desk. Its 162 rooms all came with steam heat, hot and cold running water, electric lights, and telephones. Eight corner suites had fireplaces. Rooms without bath rented for $4 and $4.50 per person,

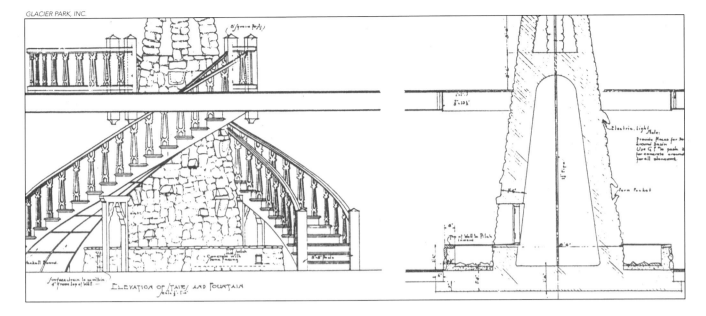

The drawing of Many Glacier Hotel's lobby staircase was typical of the detailed plans submitted for Louis Hill's approval by architect Thomas McMahon. The fountain held pockets to accommodate ferns, and arose from a pool containing fish and thirty colored lights. To stock the pool at the beginning of each season, hotel manager Omar Ellis would go on a fishing expedition, often with night clerk Ray Kinley, to catch trout from Swiftcurrent Lake with barbless hooks.

while rooms with bath went for $5 and up. All rates included meals.

The attraction of Many Glacier, though, is more than its facilities—it's in a setting that few hotels can match. Nature's wonders are right outside the door: a stone's throw away is a pristine lake surrounded by a mountain panorama that includes Altyn, Gould, Grinnell, Grinnell Glacier, Mount Wilbur, and McDermott Peak, plus trails leading to more lakes and mountains and glaciers. Ensuring guests did not miss out, the hotel provided boxed lunches on request, and had offices for row boat and fishing tackle rentals, and to facilitate trail rides.

That Many Glacier Hotel was Glacier Park's undisputed "Showplace of the Rockies" was proven that first summer: almost half Glacier's 13,465 visitors stayed at the Many Glacier facilities. Gratified Great Northern officials authorized expansion: construction of a second bedroom annex (south of the lobby) containing eighty bedrooms, and a 26-by-45-foot indoor "plunge pool" with changing rooms to the west of the dining room.

It took two full seasons to complete the $500,000 Many Glacier Hotel, which by 1918 was the largest in Montana.

While visitors have come to think of Many Glacier as just a hotel, accommodations at McDermott Lake began with a teepee village, followed by a chalet colony. Each was built incrementally and, for a period, the teepee camp, chalets, and hotel operated simultaneously, providing visitors with a choice of accommodations and prices.

Great Northern's selecting the Swiftcurrent Valley for tourism development was a natural outgrowth of its pre-park history. The area had been widely written about by conservationist George Bird Grinnell, who in 1887 first saw the nearby glacier that bears his name. In 1898 came miners who created a short-lived boom searching for copper, oil, and other minerals. Seeing the need to protect this mountain wonderland from further resource development, Grinnell, along with others, worked determinedly to establish a national park. Upon the park's creation in 1910, William Logan, the first superintendent, described the Swiftcurrent Valley as "some of the grandest scenery in the park."

Within a year Grinnell feared the result of what he had achieved in having Glacier set aside. In July he visited the region to see it again, "before it gets full of wagon roads and hotels." His timing was well chosen. That year the Great Northern erected a teepee camp at Many Glacier with ten tents to accommodate forty people. The next year, twelve log cabins were constructed to sleep and feed another 119 guests. And there was more development on the horizon.

Park officials wanted the Great Northern to build a substantial hotel

This 1915 advertisement in National Geographic extols the virtues of the newly opened Many Glacier Hotel.

85

Left: *This mid-1910s view from a stereo card shows the chalet colony at Lake McDermott and, across the creek, the recently constructed Many Glacier Hotel. The chalets were served by their own dining hall until it burned down, after which guests had to take meals in the hotel's dining room.*

Below: *Dwarfed by the mountains, Many Glacier Hotel sits on the shore of Swiftcurrent (originally McDermott) Lake. It was the largest hotel in the railway's Glacier Park chain, accommodating about 500 guests. Lake Josephine can be glimpsed in the photo's center, leading the way to Grinnell Glacier, between Grinnell Point, on the right, and Mount Allen, center. The two cabins, at the bottom of the photo near the falls, remain from the chalet colony.*

at Many Glacier. In 1913, Louis Hill, with architect Kirtland Cutter of Spokane, Washington, and the railway's own architect, Thomas McMahon, visited the lake to choose the location. Hill wanted to avoid costly mistakes of the past.

During construction of the chalet colony, government authorities had ordered the railway to tear down, relocate, and rebuild its first dining room. In March 1913, a snow slide demolished the rebuilt dining room and two other chalets. By the time the third dining room was built, the railway had incurred a loss of $7,500. It was a less-than-auspicious beginning, and Hill had no desire to see even greater losses because of poor site selection.

Construction of the hotel was threatened early on because of a feud between Hill and park superintendent James Galen over its placement. Hill said the railway would cease further investment in Glacier unless he got his way. "It is difficult enough for us to accomplish what we are trying to do in the park, building camps where there are practically no trails or roads, without expecting to meet with unnecessary opposition on your part," Hill wrote Galen. Hill received approval to locate the hotel where he wanted.

E.G. Evensta of Minneapolis was selected as contractor, and its crew of 400 began erecting a sawmill and dry kiln in the spring of 1914, cut-

Heavy snowfalls and three-story-high drifts, as seen in this May 1972 photo, are what limited winter construction of Many Glacier Hotel in 1914-15 and have since led to many of hotel's maintenance problems. The cantilevered balconies particularly suffered, and additional bracing was needed as early as the 1920s. Besides digging out the hotel each spring before opening, maintenance staff also must shovel or mop up snow that is blown inside by hard-driving wind.

ting local timber, building a bridge over the creek, and quarrying local stone.

Meanwhile, Hill immersed himself in details of architectural drawings. Hill had received two sets of drawings from Cutter in June 1914, and mulled them over for several months before rejecting both as unsuitable. They failed to incorporate the Swiss character for which Cutter was noted, and that Hill wanted. He ordered McMahon to take Cutter's drawings and revise them. McMahon kept two important features of Cutter's work: creating the hotel of three attached segments and conforming those sections to the lake shore's contour. However, McMahon revised the order of the three buildings, putting the dining room and kitchen at the north, lobby in the middle, and guest rooms to the south.

COURTESY OF MONTANA HISTORICAL SOCIETY

During his visit in August 1934, President Franklin D. Roosevelt and his entourage spent an hour and a half over lunch at Many Glacier Hotel. The president sat near a window overlooking the lake and facing the other diners. About the time of Roosevelt's visit, a suspended ceiling and hanging lights were installed in the dining room as a "modernization," covering the open beams but making the room brighter.

Hill closely scrutinized McMahon's progress on the design, even as construction was under way, insisting on all sorts of revisions. "Advise me regarding the type of flooring being considered for below the main lobby." "See me regarding the skylights in the dining room." "See me regarding the size of the chimney in the dining room." No matter was too insignificant, with Hill even fussing over whether room windows were placed low enough for guests to enjoy the views.

During the summer of 1914, workers sawed up to 14,000 feet of timber a day to build a stockpile of lumber. Other materials, such as window glass, millwork, plasterboard, shingles, and the like were transported by road from the rail line at Browning, Montana. Each load took five days to reach the building site. The route was flat, and had fewer rivers and marshy areas to cross than the Blackfeet Highway. It also freed the Blackfeet Highway for tourist travel and ensured that it remained in the best condition possible. The huge log columns used for the interior of the lobby were the exception, being shipped to Midvale by rail from the West Coast, and then transported to the site by wagons.

*"Many Glacier is the last word in mountain hostelry...Most successfully has the 'Alpine'
idea in the architecture been carried out by the elaborate yet quaint carvings noted in the
window and door frames and cornices. Very picturesque features of the structure are the
many observation galleries and 'lookout' balconies," a 1920s travel writer declared.*

Auto Stages approaching Many Glacier Hotel on Lake McDermott, Glacier National Park. Grinnell Mountain in distance.

This early postcard of "auto stages" approaching Swift-current Falls would lead travelers to believe the road from the Blackfeet Highway to Many Glacier Hotel provided a smooth and easy trip. Until the 1921 completion of Sherburne Dam to control Swiftcurrent Creek, access from Babb was problematic; heavy rains could wash away the road or leave sections boggy. The road was widened and graveled in 1916 and reconstructed in the 1920s, after the dam was built.

New Mammoth Mountain Hotel, the "Many Glacier," in th

Construction started in late summer, continuing through the fall of 1914 and into the winter. McMahon was impressed by the craftsmanship workers maintained under adverse weather conditions, telling Hill that "the detail of the stonework in the lobby…[is] exceptionally fine." That construction could continue so late in the season is a tribute to the workers' determination. At Babb, then the closest weather monitoring station, temperatures dipped to a record 53 degrees below zero in February, decisively stopping work until spring.

Eager to have the hotel opened by June but aware time was running out, Hill directed McMahon to set priorities for the completion of necessary services, forgoing others. "I think we should let the sleeping annex go, centering on the lobby and rooms around it, etc. so we can use the hotel and later finish the sleeping annex, casino, etc." McMahon replied confidently that all necessary parts would be ready for the early portion of the season. But when Hill proposed opening the hotel on June 15, anxious to impress Louis Davenport, a hotel owner of renown from Spokane expected to be in the park then, Hill was chagrined to learn it wouldn't be possible. "The new hotel cannot be completed before June 25 on account unable to get material in from

Glacier National Park, on the shores of beautiful Lake McDermott, facing Grinnell Mountain, Gould Mountain, Mount Wilbur and adjacent glaciers.

Browning," hotel company manager James A. Shoemaker wrote his boss. Poor road conditions would delay the opening another ten days.

For all Hill's involvement in the design, construction, and decoration of Many Glacier Hotel, including several on-site inspections, the last in June 1915, he ordered no special ceremony to mark the opening. On July 4, 1915, Hill was in Quebec on a salmon fishing trip.

As the Great Northern's showplace, Many Glacier Hotel had to provide the highest caliber of hospitality. The task of ensuring standards were met in those early years fell to hotel manager A.J. Binder, who later headed the hotel company. Binder "was something of a martinet and, except for employees who had duties to perform in the lobby, others were forbidden to enter it," said Warren Hanna, hotel transportation agent in 1918 and 1920. Hotel staff so feared and respected Binder that it was not unknown for employees to haul a portable gramophone a mile to Lake Josephine so they could party out of earshot of Binder and his wife, Mary.

Since the hotel is isolated, efficient operation and management were even more important than at other locations, and Binder was expected to run a tight operation, to the point that he discussed with railway officials the problem of garbage disposal. Garbage was initially burned and buried. But as early as 1915 the possibility of raising pigs was considered as a way to get rid of refuse and supply meat. Although every efficiency was examined closely, and raising animals in the park permitted

The Great Northern often employed artists to produce renderings of its hotels for their opening seasons, such as this 1915 view of Many Glacier, because there was insufficient time to clear away construction material for taking a photo. The "new, mammoth mountain hotel" was fully equipped with telephone service, a menu printer, tailor shop, infirmary with medical staff, industrial laundry machines, a 100-inch "ironer," ice house, water tower, sewer and its own electrical generation system.

The Park Saddle Horse Company's hitching posts just across from the lobby entrance of Many Glacier Hotel made access to mounts convenient. At the height of its operation, George Noffsinger's company kept 300 horses at this location, nearly one third its total. Corrals were located to the east of the hotel, in the valley below Swiftcurrent Falls, where wrangler-guides dispatched trail rides. Noffsinger, son of the saddle horse company's founder, himself managed the Many Glacier horse operation and hired others to take care of remote tent camps and smaller facilities.

under its lease, the idea was dropped. The practice of burning and burying garbage near the hotel continued, attracting bears. For many years the dump was cited in park brochures as a place to see bruins.

Most visitors to Many Glacier, however, witnessed wildlife in the wild, on one of the many saddle horse trips offered by the Park Saddle Horse Company that emanated from the hotel. The Park Saddle Horse Company had three different kinds of service: escorted camping tours known as pack tours, local rides from the hotel and back, and escorted trail tours with stops at other hotels or chalets. Morton J. Elrod, who ran some of Glacier Park's earliest ranger-naturalist programs, encouraged the wranglers, notorious for giving out misinformation, to become informed about the park. "Most tourists do not want help about riding a horse. What they want is a horse to ride and someone to tell them what they see," Elrod said.

Until the 1930s nearly every visitor to Many Glacier took a riding trip of some sort: half-day forays to Lake Josephine, or one-day trips to Granite Park, or the five-day North Circle Tour. Ironically, the wealthiest guests usually ended up paying the least. Although the Park Saddle

Horse Company was required to hand over 2¹/₂ percent of its revenues to the hotel company, hotel company managers still expected it to give VIPs—such as John D. Rockefeller, Secretary of War Henry Stimson, and writer Irvin S. Cobb—a cheaper rate than other guests.

What riders couldn't or didn't see from the saddle was covered by an interpretive program run from Many Glacier Hotel. The task of explaining nature's handiwork fell first to an independent operation under M.P. Somes who, for a fee, took visitors on guided walks. In 1922, University of Montana professor Morton Elrod provided the first free nature services. Elrod, an accomplished photographer and knowledgeable biologist, was given free rein to develop and conduct interpretive programs at Many Glacier, including lectures and guided walks.

"These trips are spoken of by tourists as red letter days in their stay and indicate the value of accompanying parties whenever it is possible to have walking guides," Elrod said in his annual report to the park superintendent. By 1924, Elrod's *Guide to Glacier*, the first comprehensive book on the park's natural features, was available for purchase. To complement these programs, the hotel company arranged for daily cultural exhibitions by the local Blackfeet.

The emphasis on nature and the unmarred beauty of the Many Glacier region gave rise to an unprecedented incident in Glacier Park history. It all had to do with the fate of Many Glacier's sawmill. Although Hill had said the mill would be torn down after the hotel was completed, it wasn't, and the Park Service continued to issue a permit for it to remain despite guest complaints that it was an eyesore. Talks dragged on for three years about what to do until a fateful day in August 1925 when Stephen Mather, director of the National Park Service, intervened, and the whole matter blew up—literally.

Mather was a man known for his mercurial temperament, but what happened puzzled everyone. Without written or verbal warning to the hotel company, Mather arrived at Many Glacier, instructed park employees to place thirteen dynamite charges around the mill, and personally pushed the plunger. When asked

Park Saddle Horse Company guide "Diamond Dick," **above**, carries lunches for a day-long trail ride. Longer trips, such as the North Circle Tour, would see the riders accompanied by packhorses to carry belongings and supplies. Great Northern publicity photo, **below**, shows a guide leading dudes and a packhorse at Dawn Mist Falls, which is on the North Circle Tour trail.

The sawmill near Many Glacier Hotel was only partially damaged by dynamite set off at the instigation of National Park Service director Stephen Mather in 1925. Mather was angry that the unused building was an eyesore amid the mountain scenery. After the explosion, park staff removed the building at government expense. Some of the salvaged equipment was later used in constructing the Prince of Wales Hotel, Waterton Park.

what was going on, Mather passed the explosions off as a nineteenth birthday celebration for his daughter.

"It was the most high-handed, unwarranted and illogical thing that has probably ever occurred in any park, and committed by a government official, is particularly deplorable," railway vice-president William Kenney said. "The only charitable way to view it is that the serious illness of Mr. Mather [some historians think it was depression] has left his mind impaired because no sane man, filling the position occupied by Mr. Mather, would ever think of doing such a thing."

Others agreed. Mather "did not talk like a sane man," said Thomas Regan, an observer of the fiasco. "I would judge from Mr. Mather's conversation that this was all done because of a personal grievance against Mr. Hill."

Louis Hill was reportedly furious, and sent lawyers to the park to take depositions from as many witnesses as possible. As tempers cooled, the matter was dropped and Hill took no legal action, very likely because the hotel company needed to curry approval for plans to increase accommodations elsewhere in the park. Meanwhile, the mill was dismantled.

The following year, 1926, brought a crisis from a different quarter. A forest fire broke out at nearby Lake Josephine, but thanks to quick action by hotel company employees and other concessioners it was contained. Exaggerated news reports of the incident and other Glacier forest fires wreaked havoc with tourism at Many Glacier. "Tourists quit preserve as timber blaze spread," read the headline in the *New York Times*. The *St. Paul Pioneer Press*, *Times*, and other papers across the country reported the park closed. The hotel company was besieged with inquiries from reservation holders wanting to know the situation.

Railway officials became livid upon hearing the reports. Howard Noble, general manager of the Glacier Park Hotel Company, protested directly to the Associated Press about its inaccuracies. Gradually, the reports were corrected and guests returned. Later, railway president Ralph Budd ordered his minions to "see that nothing like this will be repeated."

Swiftcurrent Auto Cabins, built about a mile from Many Glacier Hotel in the mid-1930s, were arranged in circles of nine to create a community atmosphere. Each cabin was equipped with a stove, wood, sink, table, cold water and electric lights. Guests had to provide their own cooking utensils or could take their meals at the nearby coffee shop. Flora and fauna were displayed in an adjacent tent museum and evening campfire entertainment was provided.

A more serious long-term threat came from the effects of the Depression. In response to the rising number of tourists traveling by car and insistence from the National Park Service on the Great Northern as its concessioner, the railroad in 1931 took the first step to considering a motel at Many Glacier. If auto-tourists weren't staying at its hotel, the railway reasoned that it could capture some of that trade with alternate accommodations. McMahon designed three types of cabins for this purpose, based on those erected in Mount Rainier National Park. The Park Service liked the proposal and approved it in July, even going as far as setting the rental rates: $2.25 per cabin a day for up to two people; $2.50 for three people and $2.75 for four. Blankets, pillows, sheets, and towels would be an additional 75 cents a day.

Despite prompt government approval, the Great Northern was hesitant. "With the country in the throes of the worst depression of its history and no prospects for improvement...spending of any money in the park by us at this time is absolutely unjustified," Kenney wrote. The plans were shelved until May 1933, when it was announced that Superior Building Company of Columbia Falls, Montana, had won the contract to erect twenty-seven cabins, at a cost of $12,297.21, about a mile west of Many Glacier Hotel.

The Swiftcurrent auto camp proved immensely popular—so much so that people were being turned away. Expansion was quickly approved, which allowed the old chalets to be taken out of use. Added at Swiftcurrent were two more cabin circles, a general store, and central shower facility. It represented an investment of more than $38,500, but in the first three years netted $10,000. The outlook seemed good, until Mother Nature came up with a plan of her own.

On August 30, 1936, a forest fire on Heaven's Peak, which everyone thought was out, was whipped up by high winds, blew across the valley to the Garden Wall and began climbing its slopes toward the Continental Divide. The next evening, as night clerk Ray Kinley prepared to go to work, he spied "two ominous, glowing red spots, like dragon eyes" near Swiftcurrent Pass, where the fire had jumped the Divide. The hotel fire alarm sounded at 10 p.m., and manager Omar Ellis notified guests that "it might be well for you to get up and pack your baggage because it's not known just what'll happen."

The fire roared down the valley toward the hotel at an unbelievable speed. Employees living in the chalets were ordered to get what belongings they could, then report to their fire duty stations. As hotel musician Donald Wheeler struggled to take a trunk and suitcase to a waiting truck, a bear charged him. Except the animal didn't attack. It ran right by Wheeler, one of many animals fleeing the blaze.

Fire crews led by head bellman Phillip March and maintenance engineer Cy Stevenson sprayed Many Glacier Hotel with a continuous stream of water. The boilers had been stoked earlier to ensure there was plenty of steam to keep the pumps running.

"The fire burned around Swiftcurrent Lake on either side of us," Kinley said. "Across the water, Mount Altyn looked like a city lit up at night. The burning pine trees were like street lights."

Employees worked through the night to ensure that embers landing on the hotel were doused. Their job was made easier because the roof consisted of fireproof asbestos-cement shingles, requested by Louis Hill in the original plans. Hill had also ordered "careful fire drills and have them at least once a week so that if [employees] should be called on they will know how to co-operate instead of getting into a panic and being useless."

By 4 A.M., the last of the employee fire crews were told they could stand down. They retreated to the lobby where they stripped off their wet clothes for blankets, and sipped hot coffee.

That morning of September 1, Ray Sleeger, head of maintenance for the hotel company, sent a coded telegram to St. Paul stating that hotel, dormitory, hydro plant, park transport garage, mess house, and water tank were still standing. Kenney sent a one-word reply: "Why?" Had Many Glacier been destroyed, the backbone of the Great Northern's hotel chain would have been gone—but so would the hotel company's

Many Glacier Hotel musician Donald Wheeler.

Hotel staff participated in weekly fire drills and learned how to operate fire-fighting equipment. At **left**, Many Glacier employees practice with a hose just hours before the Heaven's Peak forest fire roared over Swiftcurrent Pass toward the hotel on August 31, 1936. While staff was able to save the hotel, the inferno destroyed many of the newly built Swiftcurrent Auto Cabins and most of the chalets, such as the one **above** used as a hotel staff residence. All that remained of the chalets, **below left,** were the fireplaces and rocks of the foundations. Following the fire, Howard Hays, owner of the Glacier Park Transport Company, wrote to railway president William Kenney, noting: "Your Many Glacier Hotel was never so safe as it is now from forest fire. The forests around it are all consumed and for the next 30 years the only risk is from inside the hotel."

Above: For many years Many Glacier Hotel night clerks and bellboys supplemented their income by acting as fishing guides. Although they did not charge guests for this service, gratuities were accepted.

Below: Many Glacier Hotel manager Omar Ellis.

operational deficit. The blaze, however, did destroy thirty-three of the fifty-four Swiftcurrent cabins, five chalets, and the park's natural history tent museum. Only two chalets remained, near the falls.

The hotel was closed for the balance of the season as staff helped with clean-up. The next spring, Evensta Construction rebuilt thirty-one of the auto cabins. The chalets' site was returned to its natural state. The Swiftcurrent cabins were one of the few hotel company operations in Glacier not mired in red ink during the lead-up to World War II.

The postwar period was one of unease at Many Glacier Hotel as staff, management, and the railway adjusted to many changes in society. Most noticeable was the absence of the Park Saddle Horse Company, which had folded in 1943. Bernice Lewis of Browning took over the saddle horse concession at Many Glacier, but it wasn't the same. Most visitors were interested in day outings; long saddle horse trips like the North Circle Tour were but a fading memory.

Fortunately for the hotel company, Omar Ellis returned as manager after the war, ensuring some continuity in operations. The short, stocky Ellis hailed from Maine and had gotten his start at Many Glacier as a front desk clerk. He became the hotel's manager in the 1930s and remained in that position for nearly two decades. Staff feared and respected Ellis. "He was not a noticeable man, but you sure knew he was in charge," recalled bellhop Richard Rohleder of St. Paul.

One of the tasks Ellis had after the war was to discreetly see that repeat visitors and first-time patrons mingled and equally enjoyed the hospitality. The mixing, however, sometimes took a direction of its own, a situation never more interesting than at the meeting between Mrs. Oastler and screen star William Boyd, better known as Hopalong Cassidy.

New York surgeon Dr. Frank Oastler and his wife had started exploring Glacier in 1912 and became regular guests at Many Glacier. After her husband died, Mrs. Oastler, a "slightly frail Edwardian lady," continued coming each summer. "Many Glacier Hotel was Mrs. Oastler's summer duchy," bellhop Richard Schwab said. "By this time in her life her main activity was to preside as a dignified presence in the lobby when she was not in her room or at her special table in the dining room."

Her position in the lobby was jarred, Schwab said, with the arrival of the flamboyant actor and his wife, "Tripalong," Grace Bradley Boyd. Mrs. Oastler kept her distance from them, "but Hoppy, pretty well figuring it all out, effortlessly launched a campaign that completely won her over." By the time the Cassidys were ready to depart, Mrs. Oastler was part of the crowd of staff and guests to wish them farewell.

"Hopalong went over and gave her a spectacular kiss," Schwab said. "It was not some peck on a cheek for an aged aunt. It was a Hollywood kiss in which the lady is swept into the leading man's arms and bent slightly backwards....Afterward she walked around the lobby for a while in a dazed state. I was laughing so hard I think I had to go into the bellhop room so as not to make a spectacle of myself."

The new era at Many Glacier Hotel arrived full force with Donald Knutson's management contract. Knutson's renovations at Many Glacier were extensive. Outside, a porte-cochere was constructed so guests could exit vehicles in any weather without fear of the elements. Inside, the kitchen was modernized, bathrooms added to all the guest rooms, and hardwood flooring covered by tiles. Employees cursed the latter "improvement." The tiles were laid on a bed of tar that oozed up between the flooring. "Squads of summer employees used to crawl along 15 abreast, with gas-soaked rags, to clean it up," bellman John Hagen recalled.

The most noticeable changes to the lobby were removing the buffalo skulls, the Blackfeet pictographic mural, and the double-helix staircase and fountain so the gift shop could be expanded.

The Grill, in the basement of the lobby of Many Glacier Hotel, was one of the few places where hotel guests and staff could mingle (after rules were relaxed in the late 1920s). Staff often held parties there, such as this costume gala, to which hotel guests would be invited. When Prohibition ended, The Grill became a bar. Tipsy cowboys, stumbling past guest bedrooms on the Lake Level, gave the long basement hall its nickname, Stagger Alley.

Well-heeled guests mingled freely at Many Glacier, enjoying warm summer days on the hotel's lakeside porches. Each day, Blackfeet Indians performed for guests. In the evening, a park naturalist gave a lecture and showed films or slides supplied by the hotel company. Those not wishing to venture far from the comforts of the hotel could explore the grounds, where friendly chipmunks begged for food.

Bob Perkins of Wallace, Idaho, recalled working on the renovations through the winter. "We had to mix cement and it was so cold we had to heat the water with salamanders before we could pour the new cement foundation. When we tore out the stairwell, tiny bars of soap just poured out of the walls. We had three truckloads of bar soap that the pack rats had stored in the cavity of the stairway over the years. Some of them even had teeth marks on them."

Knutson's "reign of terror" ended in 1959, with the railway resuming control of the hotels in 1960. At the end of the year, Many Glacier, along with the rest of the chain, was sold to Don Hummel's Glacier Park Inc.

Under Hummel, Ian Tippet became manager at Many Glacier Hotel and director of personnel for Glacier Park Inc. The tall, lanky native of Devonshire, England, was a graduate of the London University, Westminster College. He learned about Glacier Park while working in Minneapolis on a Hilton Hotel scholarship, and was hired as assistant manager at Glacier Park Hotel in 1955.

Tippet is probably most noted for launching Many Glacier's fabled entertainment program, giving new meaning to the hotel's moniker as Showplace of the Rockies. On Monday was the Hootenanny, Wednesday the Community Sing, Thursday Serenade, Friday Skit Night, and Sunday Concert Night. There was also "Christmas in July." The showpiece of each summer, though, was a Broadway musical, premiering with "Oklahoma!" in 1961 and ending with "Kiss Me, Kate" in 1983. For the entertainment program, Tippet hired the best college music and drama students from across America for his staff. A few careers were launched from Many Glacier.

The greatest challenges Tippet faced as manager were the floods of 1964 and 1975. The June 1964 flood was the worst, with the "Lake Level" rooms taking on real meaning as water from Swiftcurrent poured into them to a level of three feet. Many Glacier was cut off from the outside world for eight days by washouts on the only road exiting Swiftcurrent Valley. Through it all, Tippet was a pillar of strength, showing the leadership for which he became renowned.

Tippet continued as manager until 1980. He remained with Glacier Park Inc. after the company was sold by Hummel, providing guidance to the new management.

The Many Glacier region today is as popular a destination as it was in 1911. The significance of the hotel to Glacier tourism was recognized when it was listed on the National Register of Historic Places. Unfortunately, Many Glacier in 2000 was in dire need of repairs. The last estimate was $50 million, an amount beyond the owners' means; they appealed to Congress for assistance. The debate was fractious, with Interior Secretary Bruce Babbitt commenting, "You know, this is a building that really ought to be torn down," a remark he later retracted.

As discussion continued about how to finance the needed repairs, sixteen rooms had the doors to the balconies permanently sealed to prevent access to the rotting structures—a black mark on the reputation of the "Showplace of the Rockies." Louis Hill would not be amused.

"For many, Swiftcurrent Lake is the hub of centers of interest to be surpassed by no other spot in the park," a National Park Service brochure boasted in 1934. "Fishing, boating, swimming, hiking, photographing, mountain climbing, horseback riding and nature study are to be enjoyed at their best here."

Its scenic location and convenient distance (a day's ride) from Many Glacier made Granite Park a prime location for chalets. The popularity of the ride over Swiftcurrent Pass and the opening of the Highline Trail linking Granite Park to Going-to-the-Sun Chalets quickly exhausted the available space at the chalets, forcing the hotel company also to maintain a tent camp at the site. Visitors were warned about the whims of the weather at high altitudes: "Be prepared for rain, high winds and freezing temperatures at any time."

— Chapter 8 —
Granite Park Chalets

G ranite Park Chalets offer guests the ultimate view with a room. The two tiny buildings sit on the edge of a high mountain plateau with a breathtaking panorama of Heaven's Peak and the Livingston Range to the southwest, the McDonald Valley to the south, and Swiftcurrent Pass and the Continental Divide to the northeast.
The highest of any chalets in Glacier National Park, at 6,690 feet, and accessible only by trail, they were named for their location. Prospectors in the 1890s working claims on Mineral Creek erroneously thought the speckled Purcell lava was granite. There is no granite in Glacier.

The decision to build at Granite Park was made late in the scheme of chalet developments. The railway waited until late 1913 before seeking a permit, and construction didn't start until 1914. There were easier, less costly places to build chalets but the scenic location, a half-day's ride from Many Glacier Valley, was irresistible to Louis Hill.

As he did elsewhere, Hill decided where to locate the first chalet. It took all summer of 1914 for E.G. Evensta's crew, under the direction of Great Northern architect Thomas D. McMahon, to finish the one-story structure. Due to the lack of local timber, McMahon designed the walls and foundation to utilize rubble masonry, with stone quarried nearby. All other building materials and furnishings were packed to the site on horses. When completed, the six-bedroom "dormitory" could accommodate eighteen guests (through the use of bunk beds).

In 1914, Samuel H. Bartlett, architect of Glacier Park Hotel, drew plans for a second, bigger chalet at Granite Park. The simultaneous construction of Many Glacier Hotel, nine miles to the east, added significantly to McMahon's workload and he was unable to design the second Granite Park structure himself. Bartlett's design contained a combination lobby/dining room, kitchen and storage area on the

RAY DJUFF COLLECTION

When the weather co-operated, guests at Granite Park Chalets would enjoy a campfire in the evenings, sharing popcorn, songs, stories and an unprecedented view of Heaven's Peak.

The original chalet at Granite Park, left, was complemented by a second one in 1915. They provided simple, rustic accommodations, with no electricity, baths, and laundry facilities. The only connection to the outside world was a phone line strung to Many Glacier Hotel over which the chalet manager would place supply orders and would receive a call each day about the number of guests expected by saddle horse. Some riders stayed only for lunch, returning to Many Glacier in the afternoon, while others continued the next day on the North Circle Tour, to Fifty Mountain Camp and Waterton Lake, or to Going-to-the-Sun Chalets on the Triangle Trip.

main floor, and eight guest rooms on the second. Work on this chalet began that summer, following completion of the first building, with laborers remaining on the job into October, when it became too cold to continue.

Ingenuity and horsepower were the backbone of the project. Angus Monroe, a guide for the Brewsters, was in charge of nine men and the eighty-horse pack strings that brought building materials over Swiftcurrent Pass from Many Glacier. It took forty-seven days just to haul in supplies, Monroe recalled. His biggest challenge was to get the large cook stove through the seventeen switchbacks leading to Swiftcurrent Pass, after others had tried and failed. Monroe and his friend, Johnny Lang, fashioned a travois to carry the stove. At each switchback, Lang dismounted to lead the horse while Monroe guided the travois. "It took us two days but we delivered it the second evening to Granite Park," he said.

By July 4, 1915, when the new building was supposed to have been finished to coincide with Many Glacier Hotel's opening, the workers were still hard at it. "Be sure and get the lumber out for the pack horses to take to finish Granite Park," Hill instructed in a July 24 telegram. "We want to rush this to completion and have no further delay." The chalet was completed in August. It was the last in the chain of chalets built by the Great Northern in Glacier Park.

The hotel company expected to operate Granite Park Chalets from

June 15 to September 15, the same schedule as its other accommodations. At this elevation, the June date proved unfeasible, and for most of its history the chalet has opened for guests early in July and closed in September, the dates always weather dependent.

Opening the chalets each summer changed little over the years. Millie Jean Perkins of St. Paul, Minnesota, who worked at the chalets from the mid-1930s to late 1940s with her mother, Ema Gunn Perkins, vividly recalled the routine. "We always arrived at Granite in a snow storm," Millie Perkins said. "An opening crew would precede us, so that when we arrived…the windows would be puttied, the screens repaired, the frames enameled white and the bedroom floors enameled a bright orange to match the muslin curtains." But sometimes winter's damage was so extensive that repairs were still ongoing. When the women arrived one year with a cook and her assistant, they found half the kitchen roof blown off.

"Both cooks looked at the mess and didn't even unpack," Perkins said. "They returned to Many Glacier on the horses that brought them up. So that year mother and I assumed the roles of cook and assistant—without a cookbook. It turned out OK."

To ensure consistency in service year after year, senior hotel company staff usually checked up on summer help and gave training tips. For the Perkinses it was general manager Adolph Aszmann. "[He] stayed overnight to give instruction on handling of groceries, linen, etc.…He showed me how to stack sheets, pillow cases and blankets with the fold on the outside for ease of taking inventory; in the bed-

The spectacular series of switchbacks on Swiftcurrent Pass, leading to Granite Park, were labeled the "Glory Trail." The pass was once known as Horsethief Pass, a route used by the Blackfeet Indians after horse raids on tribes west of the Continental Divide. It was later used by miners going from Altyn to Mineral Creek in search of copper and other precious metals. After Glacier Park was established in 1910, this trail was one of the first rebuilt with government funding.

8065—Granite Park Chalets, Glacier National Park

In the mid-1920s, twelve log guest rooms, known as "cribs," were added to the main chalet at Granite Park. The sketch below by Millie Perkins, who worked at Granite Park in the 1930s and 1940s with her mother, shows the layout of the main floor of the chalet.

room he showed me how to fold the corners of the sheets hospital style. In the kitchen, he showed the cook and helper how and where the dishes were to be stored, and in the store room how to handle and store the fresh meat and canned goods. Everything was [as] orderly as the military would require," Millie Perkins said.

In the early days, the overwhelming majority of guests arrived at Granite Park Chalets on saddle horse. Great Northern-organized bus tours of Glacier Park that lasted four days or more almost always included a horse trip and overnight stay at Granite Park from Many Glacier Hotel. The trips ensured a steady, predictable business at the chalets, and gave tour participants an unforgettable view of Glacier's grandest scenery.

Only three years after they opened, Granite Park Chalets were closed by United States entry into World War I. Besides the decline in travel, the war took its toll on the number of saddle horses available. Remounts were in great demand

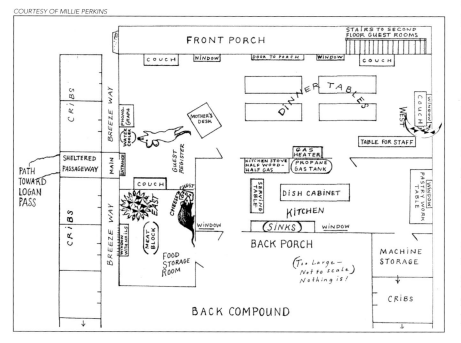

106

for the war effort, and owners sold horses to the military for much more than they could make in park tours.

Fortunately the war didn't stop trail development in Glacier and by 1919 there was a new route to the chalets: the Highline Trail that linked Granite Park to Sun Camp via Logan Pass and the Garden Wall. The trail changed Granite Park Chalets from destination to stopover for horse parties traveling between Going-to-the-Sun Chalets and Many Glacier Hotel. This soon developed into the Triangle Trip, linking all three locales via Piegan Pass.

As demand for accommodation at Granite Park grew, the hotel company added twelve rooms, known as "cribs," to the chalets. They were log sheds built as wings on either side of the main chalet. When the cribs no longer answered guest demand, the hotel company set up eighteen tents, to sleep both guests and staff. By 1927 there were beds for 144 people at Granite Park Chalets.

While the chalets' location satisfied guests' appetite for spectacular vistas, the kitchen staff satisfied their appetite for scrumptious meals. Bread, buns, and pastries were made daily, requiring long hours in the

Bus tours over Logan Pass in the 1930s bolstered the fortunes of the Glacier Park Transport Company but undermined saddle horse tours and thus business at Granite Park Chalets. The selection of bus company vehicles in this photo illustrates a period of change for the firm. Leading the pack is a touring car, one of a half dozen, long–wheel-base Cadillacs bought in 1927 to cater to small, private parties. It is followed by a White model 15-45 bus, a mid-1920s purchase to update the fleet of White model TEBs. Trailing the party is a circa 1930 White model 614 bus, which featured full side doors and a roll-back canvas top, better for inclement weather. All the buses would be replaced in the late 1930s with White model 706s.

kitchen. Preparing meals at this high altitude also required considerable skill and adaptation. The recipes used by cooks at the chalets were cherished and passed down over the years.

After an invigorating hike or ride to the chalets, the hearty cuisine was a welcomed treat. "A completely blind person could have made it to the table from a quarter of a mile away simply by following the sublime odor of bacon or ham frying and coffee simmering," Richard Schwab, a Many Glacier Hotel bellman and avid hiker, said of breakfast at Granite Park.

Although the location was informal, in the dining room the milieu was similar to that of much grander Many Glacier Hotel, but with oilcloth covering the tables. Heavy, silver-plated flatware shone beside Blue Willow plates. Fresh wildflowers formed a centerpiece at each table, and waitresses wore dark gray uniforms (later replaced by Swiss costumes). But formality only ever went so far at Granite Park and guests could usually expect, after lunch, to be invited to pick huckleberries for that night's dessert.

Millie Perkins, above left, and her mother, Ema Gunn Perkins, seated, managed Granite Park Chalets through much of the 1930s and 1940s. Ma Perkins, as she was universally known, was a former school teacher from St. Paul, Minnesota. Millie said her father, a banker, didn't mind his wife working in the mountains for the summer as it gave him time to do maintenance around the house with no one else to fuss about.

Granite Park Chalets' time in the limelight as a rest stop for saddle horse riders was brief. The beginning of the end came with the Depression and was hastened by the opening of Going-to-the-Sun Highway. Use of saddle horses fell dramatically with the onset of the economic decline, and the new road led those who could afford to tour the park to travel by car. By 1932, only $3\frac{1}{2}$ percent of visitors to Glacier were taking saddle horse trips versus 26 percent in 1926.

Granite Park Chalets survived the Depression and thrived socially, if not financially, on the strength of manager Ema Perkins. "Perkins was the epitome of sociability, loved people and was for her guests a profoundly wonderful and thoughtful person," said John Mauff of Chicago, who visited regularly. "She 'made' Granite Park Chalet."

There was already a well-established tradition of post-dinner entertainment when Ma Perkins arrived. She expanded on the variety of entertainment, leading sing-alongs, performing "readings" of tea

GRANITE PARK CHALETS, GLACIER NATIONAL PARK, MONTANA

leaves, cards, and palms, and telling chilling-but-true stories from park history.

Despite her best efforts, not everything ran perfectly. "We inherited from the previous management a handyman named Harry," Millie Perkins said. "He was not the brightest and on this particular occasion mother had asked him to replace the screen on the cheese chest in the storage room. He ran out of new screen or time, I don't know which, so with one side not enclosed he simply pushed the chest to the wall figuring that would protect the cheese from varmints....

"Mother always invited the guests after dinner to visit the kitchen so they could see how the food was preserved. On this day of Harry's venture into carpentry, mother unsuspectingly led the guests into the storage room. There was our cheese closet swarming with mice. Without batting an eye, or taking a second breath, mother explained: 'You will find this interesting. So long as we keep an ample supply of cheese with easy access for the mice, they never bother us in the kitchen.' The guests marveled at mother's ingenuity."

But no amount of hospitality could anticipate the most feared of visitors: forest fires. In 1936 a major conflagration came calling, started by a lightning strike August 18 on Heaven's Peak. Some 500 men worked several days to extinguish the blaze, or so they thought. But high winds late August 30 revived it, causing the fire to quickly crown, blowing embers off the mountain and across the valley to

When the railway's chief engineer wired Louis Hill in 1914 asking about the siting of Granite Park Chalets, Hill replied that they should be located west of Swiftcurrent Pass in the nearest convenient timber, near a good water supply with drainage, but no more than a mile west of the pass. In the end, Hill selected the site himself, ensuring guests had a clear view of Heaven's Peak across the valley.

the slope leading to Granite Park.

Throughout the next day, staff and guests watched the rising smoke with anxiety. "It wasn't until late in the afternoon that we got a message from the Park Service to leave the chalet immediately after dinner," Millie Perkins said. "Of course the guests were slowly approaching the panic stage when I served, yet in my Swiss costume, with the customary 'formality,' the usual dinner."

The wear and tear of the elements on the log construction of the cribs at Granite Park Chalets is evident in this post–World War II photo. Even with regular maintenance on the roof, windows, doors and chinking, little could be done about drifting snow that piled up against and atop the cribs, rotting the timbers as it melted. The cribs were removed several at a time over the years until none remained.

Staff and guests left about 6 p.m. carrying wet blankets to protect themselves. When they reached Logan Pass they were taken by bus to Sun Camp to spend the night. The fire overran Granite Park that evening. When she returned the next day, Ma Perkins was surprised to find the chalets untouched by fire, the path of which had miraculously split around the buildings, destroying only the two outhouses.

Granite Park Chalets were closed during World War II, reopening in 1946. With the demise of the Park Saddle Horse Company, clientele consisted almost exclusively of hikers. The fiscal and operational realities of Granite Park Chalets began to close in on the Great Northern. The cost of packing in supplies had increased significantly, making it tough to break even during the sixty-day season. The level of service the hotel company insisted be provided at Granite Park added to the cost.

Finally, in 1954, Granite Park Chalets were sold for $1 to the National Park Service, which the following year awarded the concession to Ross and Kathleen (Kay) Luding of Martin City, Montana, who had run Sperry Chalets the previous year. They reduced services to save money and increase efficiency, but much remained the same, with good food, regular visits from rangers, and nightly entertainment, including the ritual of watching from the balcony as grizzly bears rummaged through garbage that couldn't be burned. That practice would lead to tragic consequences.

In August 1967, Julie Helgeson was killed by a bear as she and com-

*Hikers and riders were attracted to Granite Park Chalets by the proximity of nearby peaks.
This party, near the summit of 7,750-foot Stanton Mountain, north of Lake McDonald, is
representative of the heights to which thrill-seekers will climb for an incredible view.*

Mount Gould and the Garden Wall are framed by the balcony of Granite Park Chalets.

panion Roy Ducat, both hotel company employees, slept in a campground near the chalets. Helgeson's horrendous death, detailed in John Olsen's compelling book *Night of the Grizzlies*, was the first fatal grizzly attack recorded in the park. Ducat, who was mauled, survived, in part because three doctors and a nurse were guests at the chalet that night.

The Luding family continued to run Granite Park Chalet (by the 1960s the name had become singular) until 1992. Increased visitation, inadequate wastewater facilities, and other problems combined to force the closure of Granite Park Chalet and its sister Sperry Chalet in 1992. Concerned citizens lobbied Congress, which allocated $3.1 million towards a total of $4.3 million to renovate Granite Park and Sperry chalets, both of which had been declared national historic landmarks in 1987.

During the four years Granite Park was closed, the chalets were extensively upgraded and repaired. Just as with the original construction, most of the material was packed in on horseback; only a few items required the use of helicopters. The chalets reopened as hiker shelters in 1996, with a limit of twenty guests a night, who are required to bring their own food and water.

Nothing can diminish the setting or the thrill of reaching Granite Park Chalet after a lengthy hike. Guests still gasp at the view from the balconies, the flagstone floors are as cold as ever, and the camaraderie around the cast iron stove just as infectious. It's one of the reasons why Glacier was voted in 2000 as the best back-country park in America by *Backpacker* magazine.

The opening of the Highline Trail along the Garden Wall in 1918 created a direct link between Granite Park Chalets, above, and the St. Mary Valley. The pathway became part of a popular Triangle Trip, connecting Granite Park, Many Glacier and Going-to-the-Sun Chalets. The Garden Wall is a huge arete, created by glaciers that gouged a broad ridge's crest into a thin, knife-edged wall. The ride along the trail from Logan Pass to Granite Park is spectacular, but not for the faint of heart or those afraid of heights.

The 90-room Prince of Wales Hotel took slightly more than twelve months to build, with work wrapping up in late August 1927 although it opened July 25 for guests with confirmed reservations. The hotel is 122 feet tall (including the 30-foot tower). About 100 train car loads of lumber and other materials were used in its construction. The main building cost $371,000, with another $300,000 spent on the water tower, boilers and laundry, staff dormitories and temporary construction buildings. Thomas McMahon's design contains many Arts and Crafts elements and made it the only hotel in the chain not to feature a "forest" lobby. One of the first Arts and Crafts societies in America was set up in Minneapolis/St. Paul and may have influenced resident McMahon's work.

— *Chapter 9* —

Prince of Wales Hotel

The Prince of Wales Hotel is by far the most picturesque in the Great Northern's chain of hostelries in Glacier National Park. The whimsical architectural style, intricate construction details, and fine woodwork set it apart from the rest just as much as its location, the only hotel of the group in Canada. The Prince of Wales Hotel is a jumble of design ideas that look very little like the original plan. But that isn't surprising since little about the hotel ever went according to plan.

COURTESY OF CONNIE HOFFMAN

At Louis Hill's suggestion, the luggage label for the Prince of Wales incorporated Canada's coat of arms.

It got off track from the beginning. Louis Hill proposed building the hotel in September 1913 during a visit to Waterton Lakes National Park, Alberta, but the idea was put on hold until 1925. The twelve-year delay was caused by factors including the outbreak of the Great War in 1914, government control of American railways in 1918 and, following that, a proposal to build a dam in Waterton that froze all building in the park for nearly three years.

Prohibition—or more correctly, Prohibition in the U.S. and the lack of it in Alberta—prompted Hill to revive the idea. A plebiscite in 1923 legalized booze in Alberta, just across the border from Glacier Park. Great Northern officials reckoned that a resort hotel in Waterton featuring a pub would boost ridership on its railway and tourism to its facilities in Glacier. After receiving tacit approval from the Canadian government, plans for a 300-room hotel—labeled a "haven for thirsty Americans" by the tabloid press—were announced, and construction began in summer 1926.

Douglas Oland and James Scott, builders from nearby Cardston, Alberta, eagerly sought the contract for the $670,000 project. They had

115

Above: Douglas Oland, top, and James Scott were the contractors who handled construction of the Prince of Wales Hotel. The Cardston, Alberta, men met in the early 1910s as tradesmen, then set up Oland and Scott Construction. The partnership lasted more than twenty-five years, interrupted only when Scott, the younger of the two, joined the army to fight during World War I. At the time they started work on the Prince of Wales Hotel, they were aged forty-two and thirty-eight, respectively.

Top right: The first month of work at the Prince of Wales Hotel site was taken up with bringing in supplies and building housing for construction workers. Digging for the foundation, above, did not begin until August 1926. A high wood fence shielded workers from Waterton's buffeting gusts, and the tower contained an anemometer to record daily wind speeds.

more than a decade's experience constructing homes and businesses in Waterton, were knowledgeable about local conditions, and willing to tackle bigger projects. The Prince of Wales Hotel would be their most famous. As with all Great Northern's building contracts, it was awarded on a cost-plus basis—in this instance, cost plus 6½ percent.

It was more than a little ironic that Oland and Scott Construction was based in Cardston. The small town, thirty miles northeast of Waterton, was founded by teetotaling Mormons, and was the only area of the province to remain dry after Prohibition.

Oland and Scott faced many challenges in their quest to complete the Prince of Wales. They overcame poor roads, inclement weather and Louis Hill's ever-changing idea about the final design, all of which extended the deadline almost two months.

Throughout the fall of 1926, the thirty-mile road between Cardston and Waterton was often a mess from repeated rain storms, melting snow, and constant traffic hauling building materials to the construction site. It was described in the local newspapers as a "sea of mud." When trucks could no longer get through, "I had to revert to horses [and wagons] and the more I hauled the worse the roads got," Oland recalled.

In the spring of 1927, Oland tried having his teamsters detour through Hill Spring to reach Waterton. It worked for a short while, until snow melt turned it, too, into a soggy mess the consistency of thick porridge. "Impossible for trucks to haul now and had two loads of lumber come in today by team that had to unload part of their loads in order to come through, the full loads sinking in up to the hubs in places," Great Northern assistant engineer Floyd Parker reported. "Had a load of lumber on the way from Hill Spring the past week that mired so deep it was impossible to pull out and was left standing. This was a four horse team outfit," Parker added.

Bad weather added to the havoc at the construction site, with rain and snow causing repeated, uncontrollable delays. "The total fall of snow was about 14 feet," Oland said. "Each time it snowed I had to lay the carpenters off and put on a crew of laborers to clear the building. Before the winter was over, I had spent $5,000 on shoveling snow."

During these layoffs workers took up shinny hockey on a rink on Linnet Lake, near their construction camp. At other times, wives and girlfriends organized basket socials and dances at the workers' mess hall. "We had a very good orchestra from the men at the camp," said Mary O'Brien, Doug Oland's daughter. "If the [band members] took a weekend off and went to Cardston or Pincher Creek, Dad would have his Victrola carried over to the cookhouse."

The worst storm of the season was the blizzard of December 10, 1926, which cut Waterton off from outside contact for nearly a week, and almost blew down the partially constructed hotel. The average wind speed was sixty-six miles per hour, with gusts over ninety, Parker reported to St. Paul, Minnesota. The wind picked up rocks, shingles, and small boards, sending them flying in whiteout conditions that made it nearly impossible to be forewarned about items falling from the sky.

"One man with a truck load of timber was just getting out of the cab on one side when a plank was driven through the window on the opposite side," *The Lethbridge Herald* reported. "He lost no time crawling under his truck until the flying timbers had landed on the ground." Others weren't so lucky, being hit or knocked down by flying lumber. Rocks picked up by the wind were "shot" through windows as cleanly as bullets.

While some of the scaffolding around the building was torn down by the gusts, the Prince of Wales Hotel survived intact, incurring only minor damage. "[I] figure the temporary six-inch by six-inch diagonal braces we placed at the west end of the east wing was all that saved this wing," Parker said. The only problem with the structure's integrity was that the wings had been blown about three inches out of plumb. Horse-

Fifty Mountain Camp, established by George Noffsinger in 1925, was strategically situated in the high alpine meadows below Mount Kipp to take in a mountain panorama. Unlike the other permanent tent camps, this one was not located near a fishing lake, but otherwise had the same amenities. Fifty Mountain Camp was an overnight stop on the popular North Circle Tour.

Right: It was during Prince Edward's 1919 trip to North America that he fell in love with the Alberta foothills and bought E.P. Ranch. Edward held onto the property for forty years, when he sold it to the Cartwright family, which still owned it in 2001.

Below: This blueprint shows the original design for the Prince of Wales Hotel before Louis Hill had the roof made steeper and added three stories to the center section.

powered winches were used to pull the building back into alignment.

An equal nuisance was Hill's repeated design changes. What Oland and Scott started building was a four-story hotel that looked very similar to the lobby section of Many Glacier. Over the course of construction, the design was radically changed. In September 1926, Hill, fresh from a summer vacation in Europe, reviewed the blueprints, learned about the poor road conditions, and ordered wholesale changes. "They are not satisfactory as to the size of rooms and arrangements thereof, or as to the exterior, and as to the general arrangements of the main building," Hill said.

He engaged the services of Beaver Wade Day, an architect with the firm of Toltz King and Day in St. Paul, to assist Thomas McMahon, Great Northern's architect, in revising the drawings. When they were finished in October, the lobby section had grown three floors to seven, under a steeply pitched roof topped by a thirty-foot tower, the eaves of the wings were lowered from the fourth to third floor, and twelve shed dormers had sprouted from steeper roofs on the wings. Any resemblance to Many Glacier Hotel disappeared in the revisions. Hill "wanted [the hotel] to look like the French and Swiss chalets he saw in Europe," Oland said.

Still, Hill wasn't satisfied. He continued meddling with the design over the next five months, requesting numerous changes, such as relocating the elevator, revising and adding fire escapes and, the most extensive of all, creating a fifth floor in the wings. The lat-

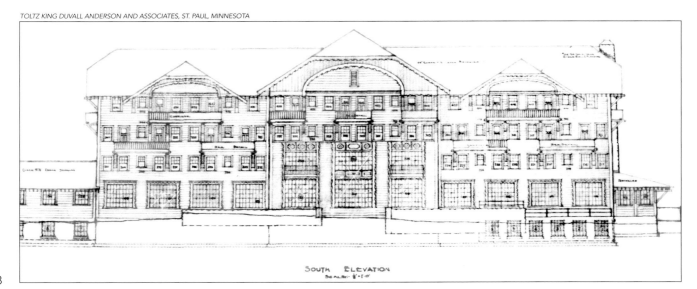

SOUTH ELEVATION
SCALE ⅛"=1'-0"

Above: Despite construction delays that hampered efforts to complete the Prince of Wales Hotel on time, the crew nonetheless found a moment in spring 1927 to stop for a group photo. Not to be outdone by the crew, on the highest beam are contractor Doug Oland and his son.

Right: This overview of the Prince of Wales Hotel construction site was taken from the 100-foot-tall water tower just six days before the 1927 opening. The outbuildings and piles of lumber remained until spring 1928 in readiness for the construction of a bedroom annex that was never approved. The buildings in the foreground are for lumber storage and a woodworking shop where carpenters cut the hotel's gingerbread moldings.

DIFFICULT TRANSPORTATION.

With roads so bad that neither trucks nor horses and wagons could get through, contractors Doug Oland and Jim Scott resorted to horse-pulled sleds to move two nine-ton boilers and two equally large fuel tanks to Waterton from the railhead in Hill Spring. A late May snowstorm aided the work, although teamsters said the sleds ran just as well in the mud when a chinook followed. As many as thirty-six horses were used to pull and push the sleds. It was such a sight that a series of pictures, of which this is one, was printed and passed around or sold to hotel workers.

ter change involved tearing apart all twelve dormers and refashioning them as gables so the room count of the hotel could be increased to ninety from seventy-eight, a process that took almost two months. Hill's tinkering "meant that a lot of the structure as it now is had been built four times [over]," Oland said.

These constant changes, combined with continued poor weather and bad roads, forced Oland and Scott to request moving their deadline from the original June 1 to June 15, then July 15.

Oland and Scott let nothing stand in their way to meet yet another new deadline, July 25. When bad roads prevented delivery of two nine-ton boilers to the site by truck, Oland and Scott improvised by placing the vessels on skids and using teams of horses to haul them in. When the combination of a burgeoning workforce—peaking at 225—overtime, and a six-day work week weren't enough, Oland and Scott got special dispensation to have their crew work Sundays.

The doors to the Prince of Wales Hotel were opened to the public on Monday, July 25, 1927. Only the beer parlor was not ready, because of a legal technicality and Hill's indecision over where to locate it. A gala dinner honoring Oland and Scott marked the opening. As was his custom, Louis Hill was not present, attending instead to business in St. Paul.

Almost immediately Hill began working on a proposal to expand the hotel's capacity by adding one or more bedroom annexes. Roy Childs Jones, another architect with Toltz King and Day, was dispatched to Waterton to draw sketches for the development. The proposal was eventually shelved, a victim of the $150,000 the Great Northern had to spend for Alberta government bonds so the province would improve the Cardston-Waterton road to all-weather status. Given a choice between adding rooms to a hotel that guests might not reach because of bad roads or spending the money on highway improvements, the Great Northern chose the latter.

Another disappointment occurred when Edward, Prince of Wales (later King Edward VIII and Duke of Windsor, after his abdication),

120

declined an invitation to visit the newly opened hotel during his 1927 tour of Canada. The prince came within thirty miles of Waterton when his train passed through Pincher Creek heading east, but Edward could not find time to see the hotel named in his honor.

The hotel had a huge impact on Waterton Park. Until then Waterton was a relative tourism backwater frequented mostly by residents of southern Alberta as a favorite, if primitive, retreat from the prairies. The Great Northern changed the quiet resort town into an international playground. It was advertised across the United States in newspapers and brochures promoting summer rail vacations. Canadians saw little of this advertising. Tourism to Waterton leapfrogged past previous records and new businesses sprang up to cater to the visitors.

Riders on the Park Saddle Horse Company's North Circle Tour, which stopped at Goathaunt Chalet at the south end of Upper Waterton Lake, added to the numbers. The chalet, the only one in Glacier Park not built by the Great Northern, was opened in 1924 by Waterton businessman Henry Hanson.

Complementing the new hotel, the Great Northern commissioned a 56-ton, 200-passenger excursion boat, the *International*, which took visitors on a tour of seven-mile-long Upper Waterton Lake. Captain William Swanson fabricated it in a shed at Goat Haunt not far from the chalet.

Louis Hill was attracted to Waterton's scenery as much as any tourist and, in 1928, apparently acting on a whim, asked Doug Oland to build a house for him in the park. For Oland, the project was like a mini-version of building the Prince of Wales, with Hill repeatedly fussing over the blueprints and changing his mind about the design for the house, which ended up costing $9,600. The two-story, six-bedroom home was completed that summer, but neither Hill nor his family ever lived in it. Oland said Hill didn't like the location, south of Cameron Falls, although Hill had previously approved the site.

Even though he didn't use the home, Hill frequently toured

Goathaunt Chalet, the most northerly in Glacier, was completed in 1924, offering only meals and supplies to hikers, riders and excursion boat passengers. Disappointing patronage forced partners Henry Hanson and Lester Morrow to sell the chalet in 1925 to the Park Saddle Horse Company which operated it until 1941 as a stop on the North Circle Tour. The building was demolished in 1952.

Head bellman Victor Harrison, right, ruled the lobby of the Prince of Wales hotel with an iron fist. He demanded a cut of all tips bellhops received for incoming luggage, but let them keep tips for other services. He probably made the most money, though, from the special license that allowed him to place personal orders for hard liquor for hotel guests. The hotel's "taproom" served only beer—an Alberta regulation until 1957 when cocktail lounges were permitted—and Waterton had no liquor store at the time.

Waterton, staying at the Prince of Wales Hotel. Staff recall Hill's whirlwind visits as hectic times—dread mixed with awe for the powerful man.

A grand scheme launched at the Prince of Wales Hotel in 1931 came to fruition the following year. Led by Canon Samuel Middleton, members of Rotary International from Alberta, Montana, and Saskatchewan unanimously passed a proposal to join Waterton and Glacier as an international peace park "to foster all international relationships." The resolution was drafted and passed by men familiar with the horrors of World War I, who saw Canada's and the United States' sharing of the world's longest undefended border as a model for other countries.

The Rotarians' proposal became reality at a ceremony in summer 1932 at Glacier Park Hotel. Since then, Rotarians have tried to meet annually, alternating between the Prince of Wales Hotel and Glacier Park Hotel, to renew their pledge of fostering peace. The first notable exception came in 1933, when Great Northern officials made the ominous decision not to open the Prince of Wales. The railway, financially strapped by the Depression, cited as its reason the cost of transporting passengers from Glacier to Waterton via Cardston.

Underlying the closure was a plea from the railway for a more direct route between the two parks, something talked about for more than a decade. Intense lobbying by the railway, backed by park officials, prompted the governments on both sides of the border to approve constructing the Kennedy Creek cutoff (now Chief Mountain International Highway) as a Depression make-work project. When the road was completed in 1936, the Prince of Wales Hotel reopened, and Rotarians were able to hold the follow-up peace park ceremony put off for three years.

The hotel's re-opening was also great news for Alberta youths looking for work. Peggy Dederick had been laid off as a salad girl at the Palliser Hotel in Calgary, Alberta, due to the Depression, and was glad to get a summer job at the Prince of Wales, initially washing glasses and silver-

Above: *A touring car and three accompanying Glacier Park Transport Company buses carrying Howard H. Hays, Sr., and other Glacier Park dignitaries pull up to the front doors of the Prince of Wales Hotel on opening day. The flagpoles decorating the north side of the building were a last-minute addition by Louis Hill, after he found an eight-foot-high weather vane had been mounted on the tower where he had hoped to put a flagpole.*

Right: *Pictographs painted by members of the Blood Tribe decorate walls behind the front desk and lanterns suspended at various heights throughout the lobby. Photographs of the native artists would later be placed by each panel along with an explanation of the symbols. Modernization of the lobby in the late 1950s saw the lanterns and pictograph panels removed. Some lanterns were used in the lobby of Lake McDonald Lodge; some panels are on display at Fort Museum in Fort Macleod, Alberta.*

Guests using the Prince of Wales Hotel dining room always wanted to be seated near the windows so they could gaze out at seven-mile-long Upper Waterton Lake and its surrounding peaks. For those without a view, on the walls were oil paintings by John Fery of scenes from Waterton and Glacier parks. Place settings featured Blue Willow china, and silverware with the initials of the Glacier Park Hotel Company or Canadian Rockies Hotel Company. The plates and cutlery were used until the 1980s.

ware, and later making salads and desserts.

One of the kitchen staff's frustrations was two bears, Maggie and Jigs, that perpetually raided the garbage cans, spilling their contents and making a mess. "The chef got us all together to make buns up and smear them with all kinds of hot stuff," Dederick said. "That night, when it was dark, we…arrived in cars and waited until the bear came. Well, he let out one big roar and jumped over the verandah. We were hoping no one would be in his path. He was one angry bear."

At the hotel's helm was manager Harley Boswell. The native of Peoria, Illinois, had a distinguished career at the Prince of Wales Hotel that spanned nearly three decades, starting in 1930. It was a summer job for Boswell and his wife, Anna, head of the housekeeping staff; in the fall Boswell returned to his position as an assistant manager at the Palmer House in Chicago. During the latter half of the Depression years, Boswell did much to resurrect business at the Prince of Wales, especially after it lost its position as a "haven for thirsty Americans" with the 1933 repeal of Prohibition in the U.S.

Boswell's personal touches, such as having a bottle of a returning guest's favorite beverage in his room, along with a bouquet of flowers, helped build a coterie of guests who would return each summer for decades to come.

Returning tourists had to break routine in 1942, however, when the Prince of Wales Hotel failed to open. The closure was the result of wartime fuel restrictions in Canada, which had entered the war in 1939, and Great Northern's unwillingness to convert the hotel's boilers to burn coal. The hotel remained shuttered until the summer of 1946.

Again, Boswell returned, bridging the gap of time for guests and ensuring that new patrons received the same high standard of service as before the war. Boswell resumed his role as master host as if the four years of closure had not existed.

"I can recall that after I left Waterton in the fall of 1932, I never returned till about 25 years," said bellhop Ainslie Pankhurst of Lethbridge, Alberta. "I walked into the hotel in the summer and Mr. Boswell was at the front desk. He said: How are you, Ainslie?

"I nearly flipped. I was so surprised that he would remember my name after all those years. He must have dealt with hundreds of employees in those years....A great hotel man. He had a way with guests."

Boswell's run as manager ended in 1957 when Donald Knutson managed the hotel chain. As at the other hotels, the Prince of Wales

Great Northern officials refused to use the term Waterton-Glacier International Peace Park in company promotional brochures because they deemed it awkward, and Glacier Park played second fiddle in the title. Rather, they printed postcard booklets like this, which had Glacier first in the title but showed the Prince of Wales Hotel in Waterton. The booklet included the above Tomer Hileman photo of the Prince of Wales Hotel lobby windows.

Completed in September 1927, the International began excursion cruises in 1928 on Upper Waterton Lake. It ferried not only sight-seeing guests from the Prince of Wales Hotel but also trail riders from Goathaunt camp. During the 1930s, midnight cruises were run from Waterton to Glacier so partiers could Alberta skirt laws prohibiting dancing and drinking on Sundays. The International is still in use today.

came in for a series of major overhauls and upgrades during the Knutson years. All the kitchen equipment was replaced, new furniture was ordered for the rooms, the Dominion Suite was created by combining two rooms on the third floor, a fire suppression sprinkler system was installed throughout the building, the lobby remodeled, gift shop expanded, and the beer parlor closed, replaced by a cocktail lounge fashioned out of the lobby's east wing.

The revamp destroyed much of the hotel's original decoration, removing John Fery oil paintings in the dining room, replacing Blood Indian pictographs in the lobby with wallpaper, cutting up the grand staircase for the lounge, and junking the variable-height lobby lanterns for a three-tiered aluminum chandelier. The upgrading did serve to attract a buyer for the hotel—Don Hummel and Glacier Park Inc.

In the 1960s, Hummel toyed with the idea of expanding the Prince of Wales Hotel into a convention center. The expansion would have been mostly underground, with meeting rooms that had windows cut into the cliff facing south, overlooking Upper Waterton Lake. Proposed changes to federal legislation regulating leaseholds that would have made it uneconomical to invest in improvements brought a swift end to any expansion plans.

In 1981 Glacier Park Inc. was sold to a company that would

Left: The east wing of the lobby of the Prince of Wales Hotel has been extensively remodeled since this 1927 picture was taken. The room was divided in 1959 to expand the gift shop, and the fireplace was redesigned for the Windsor Lounge. Enjoying the fireplace before the renovations are Captain R. Stanley Harrison, the hotel's first manager, and five-year-old Margaret Moores, daughter of chef Len Moores. When hired, Moores and his wife, who worked as a maid, never told Harrison they were bringing Margaret. Fortunately, Harrison took a shine to the tyke and doted on her, as did the rest of the staff.

Below: Quaint amenities, such as a sink and mirror in the bedroom, that have not been modernized were among the reasons the Prince of Wales Hotel received designation as a historic site in the 1990s.

become known as Viad, and another series of upgrades were completed over several years. Among the changes were installing a new roof over the original cedar shingles, expanding and remodeling the gift shop, retiring the boilers and replacing steam heating with electrical radiators in each room, installing modern windows in guest rooms, and replacing the Dominion Suite with two new luxury rooms.

For its unique role in Waterton's history and as an outstanding example of railway mountain architecture, the Prince of Wales Hotel was declared a national historic site in 1995. The designation soon played a role in a decision by a Canadian government panel to reject a proposal to expand the building by adding bedroom annexes similar to those Great Northern officials had contemplated seventy years before. It would appear, unless the winds of politics shift drastically, that the distinctive profile of the Prince of Wales Hotel will not be altered materially in the foreseeable future.

On dark nights, guests who dawdled too long over supper or stayed to play cards and trade stories needed a lantern to walk from the Sperry Chalets dining hall, foreground, to the distant sleeping quarters. The attraction of the chalet colony has not changed since the day it was constructed: relatively easy access to nearby Sperry Glacier. However, the metal ladder up the cliff that visitors were required to climb to reach the glacier was sometimes more than some trekkers could manage.

— *Chapter 10* —

Sperry Chalets

Sperry Chalets are situated in the "land of goats and glaciers," on the precipice of a glacial cirque 6,560 feet above sea level. The location is not only devastatingly beautiful, but also strategic. It was picked by the Great Northern both as a gateway to its accommodations to the east and to control access to Sperry Glacier, one of the most popular tourist destinations in the early history of Glacier National Park.

Sperry Glacier was named for Lyman B. Sperry, who first reached it in 1896. A professor of geology and zoology at Carleton College in Minnesota, Sperry was enticed to explore the Glacier Park region by a Great Northern passenger agent who asked him to "make such observations as you shall find practicable regarding our scenic attractions." It was the first hint of the railway's interest in developing tourism in Glacier—more than a decade before the area became a national park.

Sperry's "discovery" of the glacier made it an instant attraction, although access was not easy due to its location up a steep cliff. To improve accessibility, Sperry appealed to J.J. Hill, who agreed to sponsor construction of a trail from Lake McDonald over Gunsight Pass to St. Mary Lake, with a spur to the glacier. Sperry got fifteen of his students to do the work, with the railway providing free transportation to the park, the food, tents, and supplies. Completed in 1902, the trail was frequently used by guests at Lewis's Glacier Hotel on Lake McDonald.

In proposing a chalet colony near Sperry Glacier, Great Northern officials hoped to reap some of what they had sown a decade before in sponsoring construction of the Gunsight Pass trail. For the first two summers, 1911 and 1912, visitors to Sperry Glacier had to be content with a tent camp. Proof of the glacier's popularity as a destination was affirmed by the guest count: 461 people in 1912, second only to that of the Gunsight Lake camp.

During 1912, a small crew of Italian stone masons built a 22-by-80-

RAY DJUFF COLLECTION

Riders between Sperry and Cut Bank chalets couldn't help but be impressed by the sight of Gunsight Lake. Gunsight Chalets, hugging the shore, let visitors revel in Glacier's remote wilderness. They were within easy reach of a trail leading to Blackfoot Glacier (see photo, page 79). The colony included a two-story bedroom building and dining room–kitchen. The buildings were constructed in 1911 from local timber. After an avalanche destroyed the chalets in March 1916, they were never rebuilt.

foot stone kitchen and dining hall near the tent camp. Location dictated the choice of building materials, and they made the most of rubble stone that was at hand. Loggers who specialized in timber framing harvested the humble fir and lodgepole pine native to the area for the building's rafters. Other building supplies were brought in by horses on long pack trains originating from Sun Camp.

The dining hall was ready to serve guests in 1913. That same summer work began on a two-story, twenty-four-bedroom dormitory. The 32-by-90 building was designed by architect Kirtland Cutter of Cutter and Malmgren in Spokane, Washington. Like the dining hall/kitchen, it was constructed of native rock. Ever mindful of operational efficiencies, Louis Hill—five days before the facility was completed—inquired of staff if a laundry was needed. "I am sure we do not need to provide this," he concluded for himself. His reasoning was that since lumber was difficult to come by on site, it would be too expensive to build.

When the complex opened in 1914, Sperry Chalets was capable of housing 152 guests; the guest dormitory holding seventy-five (using bunk beds), and the tent camp sheltered the remainder. The tent camp was dismantled during World War I.

The feature of the chalets was hospitality, since it offered few of the airs of civilization, being so far in the wilderness. Guests could rent private rooms or share accommodation with other visitors. The bedrooms were lit with kerosene lamps, and their sinks had cold running water from a small reservoir on a creek behind the chalet. Hot water could be requested for delivery. A stove in each wing of the dormitory supplied heat. Since digging toilets in this rocky terrain was nearly impossible, the outhouses had fifteen-gallon cans with toilet seats. Human waste and kitchen refuse were disposed of over the cliff. This convenient solution would, decades later, force the chalets' closure.

What the chalets lacked in amenities the staff tried to compensate for with wholesome meals. Menus and available supplies were always carefully coordinated. Any shortages were made up with plenty of freshly baked bread. Mary Roberts Rinehart noted this when she arrived at the chalet in 1915 after many days on the trail: "No more ham and coffee over a wood fire, the cutting of much bread on a flat stone," she wrote of Sperry.

Although Sperry Chalets are only seven miles—but up a steep grade—from the dock at Lake McDonald where a supply boat landed daily, they were, until 1930, supplied from Going-to-the-Sun Chalets ("Sun Camp"), fifteen miles to the east. Supplies were carried by truck from Midvale (East Glacier) to St. Mary Chalets, taken by vessel to Going-to-the-Sun Chalets, and then transferred to pack horse for the long trip to Sperry.

Not coincidentally, most tours to Sperry originated from Sun Camp, ending at the Glacier Hotel on Lake McDonald. For a few years the trip was broken by a stop at Gunsight Lake, where the Great Northern had another tent camp and a short-lived chalet colony.

Using Sun Camp as a staging area to supply Sperry and as a link in tourist trips ensured Great Northern's control, much to the dismay of John Lewis, owner of what is now Lake McDonald Lodge. Lewis was unhappy that the Great Northern used the chalets to lure tourists away from extended stays at his establishment, recommending that patrons visit eastern areas of the park where the railway had its hotels. Never mind that Lewis was the beneficiary of Great Northern-organized tours of trail riders heading west over Gunsight Pass, far greater in number.

The animosity flared in 1929 as the Great Northern tried to buy Lewis's hotel and

Above: *Dr. Lyman Sperry is the namesake for Sperry Glacier and was one of the early promoters of creating Glacier National Park.*

Below: *Guest dormitory at Gunsight Lake.*

The guest dormitory at Sperry is the only one of the Great Northern's chalets in Glacier to carry such a visible and long-lasting corporate marker: GNRy. The reason is not known. During 1990s reconstruction of the chalets, the right corner of the dormitory was excavated to improve drainage. The floor joists originally rested on bedrock, some being scribed and cut to fit the location, which led to water damage and rotting each spring when the snow melted.

he resisted, demanding a higher price than the railroad was willing to pay. Lewis had his staff take revenge by telling tourists they could not get a decent meal or accommodation at Sperry Chalets so they had better take one of Lewis's boxed lunches and plan on camping or making only a day trip. People who had prepaid rooms waiting at Lewis's were reluctant to write off the cost and stay overnight at Sperry instead when they learned the truth.

Lewis "pretty near ruined our business" at Sperry that season, railway vice-president William Kenney moaned. The bickering ended in February 1930 when Lewis finally accepted Great Northern's offer. The railway immediately switched its supply trains to originate from Lake McDonald Valley and began rebuilding business at Sperry Chalets, promoting daily round trip rides from Lake McDonald Hotel for $5.

Sperry Chalets, like its counterparts, suffered during the Depression as visitation to the park dropped off. Adding to the decline was completion of Going-to-the-Sun Highway in 1933, which opened Glacier's interior to automobiles, ending the monopoly of saddle horse tours on sightseeing in remote areas. Nonetheless, Sperry was one of only three back-country chalets never closed during the 1930s. In view of reduced visitation, the number of guests that could be accommodated here was cut from seventy-five to forty-five by replacing bunk beds with twin beds.

Jeanne Fischer of St. Paul, Minnesota, who spent the 1932 season at Sperry as a maid/waitress, said only 112 people visited all summer. "We started out with a crew of seven, but there were so few people going through that one couple was sent home." Among the few guests was the Frick family of Carnegie Frick steel. The parents each brought a personal secretary and "about 18 pieces of luggage," Fischer said. But it was the Fricks' son who garnered the most attention. The boy, about eight, caught a mouse at the chalet and insisted on taking it on to Lake McDonald. "The guide said, No. Mr. Frick said, Yes. The guide said, No, and pointed out that the mouse, jumping around in the five-gallon gas can in which it had been placed, would upset the horse," Fischer said. "The child threw himself down on the ground and had hysterics, but the guide won."

Sperry Chalets remained open through the summer of 1942. None of the hotels or chalets was open for the summer of 1943, and they remained shuttered until the summer of 1946.

The role of Sperry Chalets changed after World War II. With the Park Saddle Horse Company out of business, the chalets catered primarily to hikers. This prompted park officials to initiate an overnight hike to Sperry led by a park naturalist. As before, the dining hall was the central meeting place, where guests lingered after meals, strolling out later in the evening to watch the sun set from the balcony or chat about the day's events.

Ensuring Sperry Chalets' smooth operation in the late 1940s was

A small lounging area complete with a wood-burning heater was located at the two main-floor entrances to the guest dormitory. At one time, the separate entrances were for women and men, who shared bedrooms on either side of the building. The bedrooms look much the same today as they did when the dormitory was finished in 1914, even featuring the original metal beds.

Ross Luding gives his wife Kathleen and their son Lanny a hug at the start of the 1954 season, their first, at Sperry Chalets. Ross Luding, a Montana native, had been a mess sergeant in the U.S. Army, serving in Italy during World War II. Ross worked only one season at Sperry, taking a job as a maintenance electrician at Anaconda Aluminum's Columbia Falls reduction plant the next year. Management was left to Kathleen (known as Kay to everyone), and a chef was hired to replace Ross. Kay managed Sperry until the mid-1980s.

manager Martha Russell. She was an outgoing and warm person who "made all the difference" in guests' satisfaction. There was apparently a friendly rivalry between Russell and Ema Perkins, the manager of Granite Park Chalets, to see who could finish the season with the least deficit. The competition was never overt, recalled guest John Mauff of Chicago, but each woman felt it important to earn patrons' admiration, because many guests, like Mauff, visited both establishments, and comparison was inevitable. What neither manager skimped on was meals, and at a rate of $2.50 for supper or as part of the $9.25 American plan charge, guests could expect huge portions. Mauff recalled being invited to carve a turkey as the evening's piece de resistance. "In came a 23-pound roast turkey," he said. "Yeah, man, we feasted that night. It was typical of what one could expect."

The cost of maintaining such service, along with the need for constant repairs, and decreasing guest numbers during the short, sixty-day, operating season, was extremely high. Combined with a dwindling percentage of rail arrivals in Glacier, the hotel company began in 1948 to seriously examine its ownership of Sperry and other park accommodations. The Great Northern signaled its lack of enthusiasm in 1953 when it quit serving meals at the chalet. The next year, the hotel company sold Sperry Chalets to the National Park Service for $1.

In March 1954, the Park Service approached Ross and Kathleen (Kay) Luding about operating Sperry and Granite Park chalets. "Dad agreed to try operating Sperry for a year, but not Granite," said son Lanny Luding.

If the Ludings were to make a go of it, they had to abandon many of the extravagances of Great Northern times. "The first change Dad implemented was to get a Maytag gas-powered washing machine packed up and do the laundry at the chalet," Lanny said. Previously linens were taken by pack horses for laundering at Lake McDonald Hotel. The first summer netted the Ludings less than $300, but the lure of the mountains and the variety of experiences encountered in the work convinced them to try another season. Kay Luding would return for more than thirty summers as manager of Sperry Chalets, with Ross keeping a full-time job outside the park and running supply missions on weekends.

Kay Luding's love of Sperry Chalets was in the variety of people she'd meet, said Lanny. None was more outstanding than Mrs. T.O. Court and her burro, Uranium, who arrived on their doorstep the second summer Kay managed Sperry. Court, a sixty-four-year-old Oregonian who went by the nickname Grandma Walker because of her love of hiking, used Uranium to carry her pack and supplies everywhere she traveled in Glacier. The two were inseparable, so much so that when Court was out of sight Uranium would bray until she returned. Court thought the burro might settle down in the evening during their overnight stop at Sperry, but Uranium didn't, and neither she nor other guests could sleep because of the noise. Finally, Court gave up her bed, and spent the night outside sleeping beside the burro.

After Ross's death in 1979, Lanny took over organizational and maintenance duties. The comfortable routine Lanny Luding had gotten into running Sperry was upset in late 1992 when the chalets were ordered closed until a solution was found to water quality problems. By the 1980s, nearly 200 people a day were visiting Sperry, all of who needed to use the toilet. The handling of waste had changed little from when the chalet first opened—it was still being dumped over the side of the cliff. The toilet facilities had been replaced with flush toilets in 1964 linked to concrete tanks that also held wastewater from the laundry and kitchen. Studies found the dumping and other measures were causing environmental imbalances.

The dining hall and kitchen was the first permanent building constructed at Sperry Chalets. Still in use today, the cash register was carried up the mountain along with other building supplies on packhorses. The pantry is lined in stainless steel to prevent critters from trying to gnaw their way through the floorboards and joists.

135

Described in park literature as one of the finest spectacles of the Rocky Mountains, Sperry Glacier is located just two and a half miles from the chalets. Hikers were advised to wear "sturdy shoes, preferably hob-nailed...and exercise extreme caution to avoid crevasses and patches of soft snow." The Park Saddle Horse Company provided expert guides for exploring the glacier, at no additional charge.

The cost of ending the problem was estimated in the millions of dollars.

In response, a group of Montanans formed Save the Chalets, a group dedicated to raising $1.2 million. In the end, Congress deemed restoration and reopening of the chalets "a critical investment," eventually appropriating $3.1 million to renovate Sperry and Granite Park chalets. Much of the money was spent on what the media dubbed a "$1 million toilet," which resolved the Sperry water pollution issue but garnered brickbats because of the "outrageous" construction cost, a factor of the remote location and attempts to be environmentally sensitive.

Sperry Chalets were reopened in 1999, with Lanny Luding back as concessioner. It was the toughest opening he'd ever undertaken. Since all supplies and utensils had been removed during reconstruction, "we had to replace everything," Luding said.

Sperry remains today as active and bustling a hostelry as it ever was. It is a holdover from the era before Going-to-the-Sun road opened a great swath of the interior of Glacier Park to cars, when the only way to see the remote wilderness of Glacier was on horseback. Renovations have ensured Sperry will be accessible to Glacier Park visitors for generations to come.

Sunny afternoons allowed guests at Sperry Chalets to relax out-
doors and enjoy views of Lake McDonald, to the west, and moun-
tain goats that frequented surrounding cliffs.

John Lewis, who hunted regularly and traded furs with locals before Glacier became a park, may have personally bagged many of the mounted animals on display in his hotel. He and his wife Olive were particularly proud of the lobby's quaint and cozy atmosphere. E.S. Bryant of Kalispell did much of the taxidermy for Lewis, also regularly cleaning the displays. In October 1999, eight of the deer heads, two antelope heads and a polar bear skin rug were stolen.

— *Chapter 11* —

Lake McDonald Lodge

No hotel or chalet site in Glacier Park has historic foundations as deep as those at Lake McDonald Lodge. Visitors wrongly tend to think of it as one in the series built by the Great Northern Railway in the park. With its beautiful, open beam log lobby, huge, inviting fireplace, and magnificent lake-side setting, that's understandable, but the lodge was not Louis Hill's brainchild. Hotelier John Lewis commissioned the building at the same time the railway was building its hotels.

The lodge's origins, however, precede Great Northern's days in the park. Tourists have been flocking to its site since 1895, the year George Snyder built and opened his Snyder Hotel at the very same spot. Snyder's was a two-story frame building with twelve rooms, fronted by a porch where visitors could watch the flare of sunset across the head of the ten-mile-long lake.

The first settlers in the Lake McDonald region arrived after the "discovery" of Marias Pass by John F. Stevens in 1889. Men such as Snyder, his neighbor Frank Geduhn, Denny Comeau, Milo Apgar, and Charlie Howe had no problem obtaining title to their properties on the lake; creation of Glacier Park was fifteen years in the future, and the land was open for homesteading.

Within a few years came signs of a nascent tourism industry as passengers detrained at Belton to make their way to the lake. By the time Snyder built his hotel, there was a small but steady stream of tourists—mostly from Columbia Falls, Kalispell, and other Montana communities to the west. Prospectors also passed on their way to the "ceded strip," land east of the Continental Divide that the U.S. government bought from the Blackfeet to open for mining.

Since there was no road to Snyder's hotel, he and Frank Kelly purchased a forty-foot steamboat, the *F.I. Whitney*, and had it hauled by rail and over trail to Lake McDonald from Flathead Lake.

The big attraction for guests at Snyder's was a visit to Sperry Glacier.

SADDLE HORSE TRIPS from LAKE McDONALD HOTEL

GLACIER PARK HOTEL COMPANY

Brochures such as this were distributed during the Depression to try to encourage visitors to see the backcountry from that special vantage point only a horse could provide.

This circa-1930 photo of newly renamed Lake McDonald Hotel was reproduced for decades by the Great Northern. Interestingly, it shows a Rockies panorama, with Mount Brown dominating, and downplays the lake, which intrudes on the left. Earlier images were invariably taken from the lake, showing water in the foreground, a boat or two, the hotel and a mountain backdrop. Prior to the opening of Going-to-the-Sun road, the lakeside was considered the "front" of the hotel. Since the road's opening, there have been repeated attempts to spruce up the "back."

Its deep crevasses and blue-green ice, nine miles away and 3,300 feet up the mountain, are impressive. "It matters not how one gets there, the visit to Sperry Glacier is an event of a lifetime," Margaret Thompson advised in her book *High Trails of Glacier National Park*. "No other combines such a richly filled panorama of scenery with study of glacial phenomena."

Snyder maintained his seasonal resort on Lake McDonald until 1906, when ownership of the hotel and surrounding land was transferred to John and Olive Lewis of Columbia Falls. A number of tales surround the deed's transfer. The most popular has it that a drunken Snyder lost the hotel to Lewis in a cut-throat poker game. Others have speculated that Snyder was tired of the isolation, and wanted out. The reported value of the deal was $1,500.

Olive and John Lewis were experienced hotel owners when they picked up Snyder's summer resort. A Columbia Falls lawyer, John Lewis was better known as the owner/operator of the Gaylord Hotel and of the J.E. Lewis Fur Company that traded with local trappers and natives.

Lewis took over the hotel at a critical juncture in the Glacier region's

DINING ROOM, GLACIER HOTEL.
LAKE McDONALD, MONT.

development. There was lobbying to turn the area into a national park, and Lewis got caught up in the promotion and a tourism boom that coincided. The year after he acquired the now renamed Glacier Hotel, Lewis began constructing thirteen cabins, still in use today north of the building. A room was $3 per night.

Lewis was a commanding figure in any crowd, and very gregarious. He was a Mason, and a member of the Odd Fellows, Elks, Kiwanis, and Modern Woodmen of America. He was quick with a smile and anecdote. If prompted, he'd happily recall his single season as a catcher with a professional baseball team in Helena, Montana.

Business flourished as word of Lewis's hospitality spread. He soon found himself adding more facilities: an infirmary in 1909, and Snyder Hall in 1911. The hall was used for dances that Lewis hosted. He also ran a small store dispensing staples and mail to local residents.

The camaraderie that pervaded the tourism industry around Lake McDonald changed with creation of Glacier National Park in 1910, and Great Northern's launching of its hotel and chalet building program. The immediate impact was the end of Lewis's involvement in the fur trade. No longer could he or his neighbors run trap lines and trade with local Indians, filling a hotel storeroom with furs that Lewis took to New York to sell each year. But the long-term effect concerned Lewis and other hoteliers more: Louis Hill and his railway were threatening their livelihoods. Belton and Sperry chalets were direct competition to the loyalty of the clientele Lewis and the others had been building for fif-

The dining room at the Lewis (Glacier) Hotel served the usual fare, plus a few house specialties such as locally caught salmon and trout and, as a result of owner John Lewis's hunting expeditions, wild game such as bear, moose, deer and goat. The Lewises ensured their hotel matched the standards of the Great Northern's facilities, enhanced by congenial host John Lewis's astute pandering to celebrities who frequented his establishment.

Glacier Park Transport Company began taking tour buses up the western side of Going-to-the-Sun Highway in the late 1920s, making regular trips from Lake McDonald Hotel to the summit at Logan Pass as soon as the road was completed that far. The transmountain road was a reason Howard Hays cited for getting back into the concession business in 1927 and buying the red-bus company from Roe Emery. Some 23,000 vehicles passed through the western entrance of Glacier Park when the first leg of Going-to-the-Sun road was opened in 1929—compared to 5,600 through the St. Mary entrance, on the east side of the park, during the same period.

teen years.

Lewis, with his greater financial resources, was in a better position than Apgar, Howe, and Geduhn to take on the Great Northern. Lewis might not have been able to beat Hill, but at least he could defend himself. In 1913, he contacted the architectural firm of Cutter and Malmgren to design a new hotel to replace Snyder's original building.

In selecting architect Kirtland Cutter, Lewis found someone worthy of the task of creating a Swiss-style building to rival the Great Northern's. Cutter, who had set up his Spokane, Washington, practice in 1889, had studied houses in the Bernese Oberland area of Switzerland, and proven his ability by creating the award-winning Idaho Building at the 1893 World's Columbian Exposition in Chicago. Cutter's own home was also in Swiss chalet style.

To make way for construction, the Snyder building was moved back and turned into a general store. Workers cut spruce and fir trees near Snyder Creek, piling up thirty cords of shake bolts and almost 5,000 board feet of lumber. Construction went on throughout the winter of 1913-1914, taking ten months to complete. Lewis contracted a string of pack horses and mules to get material from Belton to the lake, where the *Whitney* pulled a barge to the site. Later, when the lake froze, the pack animals hauled supplies over the ice. Lewis is reported to have spent $10,000 on freight.

Lewis's Glacier Hotel was unveiled to the public on June 14, 1914, at a gala attended by 500 people. "With all due respect to Louis Hill and

Fireplace Lewis Hotel

his corps of Glacier Park architects and designers," *The Columbian* newspaper reported, "the new Hotel Glacier on Lake McDonald…not only equals the beautiful Midvale structure in every way, but goes it about one point better.…

"The Lewis hotel stands out from its rival by virtue of the fact that a lady attended to the buying and installation of the furnishings. Mrs. Lewis has selected with a lavish hand and artistic taste and given to the place an air of homeiness [*sic*] and cheeriness that man fails to give in such work."

Olive Lewis reportedly spent $12,000 on furnishings, bringing the final price of the hotel to $68,000. The new hotel and the now twenty cabins had a total of sixty-four guest rooms, many equipped with private baths.

Whether Louis Hill liked it or not—and he didn't—his railway would have to contend with Lewis. Great Northern brochures always included Lewis's hotel, but were circumspect, listing it as a stop between Belton and Sperry chalets. Details were kept to a minimum.

This studied indifference went as far as rejecting an overture from Lewis in late 1914 to sell his recently completed hotel. "[Hill] said it would be all right if any one else wishes to purchase it from Lewis, but it is something we do not want to take over," a railway official noted. What prompted the offer is unknown. However, that summer there had been a definite animosity between the railway and Lewis, with the latter telling his employees to discourage links with Great Northern's

The huge dimensions of the fireplace at the Lewis (Glacier) Hotel are hard to gauge in this 1920s era postcard. It is twenty feet wide, twelve feet deep and seven-feet tall. Rumor persists that cowboy artist Charlie Russell drew the native-style etchings surrounding the fireplace. Russell was often a visitor here, and the tale likely was perpetuated by hotel staff after the Great Northern's takeover to add to the building's character.

A special tab was cut in Lake McDonald Hotel menus so staff could insert a small branch of aromatic cedar. It made a great keepsake for guests, and helped promote riding tours from the hotel, such as trips to Trail of the Cedars, Avalanche Lake and, for the more adventurous, Sperry Chalets and the nearby glacier.

hotels.

The symbiotic relationship between Lewis and the railway worked heavily in Lewis's favor. For the most part, Lewis was happy to go along, even incorporating the railway's "See America First" slogan on his hotel stationery. Mary Roberts Rinehart's book *Through Glacier Park—Seeing America First With Howard Eaton* is an example of how, despite the fact the 1915 tour was partly subsidized by the Great Northern, there was no way to avoid mentioning Lewis's, which, as for so many other riding tours here, was the final stop.

The presence of well-known personalities like Rinehart added to the interesting milieu at Lewis's. "Johnny Lewis…used to entertain a lot," recalled Charlie Jennings, a homesteader and summer packer. "I guess they used to have some parties." The celebrities included musicians Powder River Jack and Kitty Lee, Senators Thomas Walsh and Burton K. Wheeler, artists Joe DeYoung and Olaf Seltzer, and humorists Irvin S. Cobb and Will Rogers.

The most renowned and regular visitor was cowboy artist Charles M. Russell. He and wife Nancy had a cabin, named Bull Head Lodge, at Lake McDonald. "Charlie often rowed his boat to Apgar to pick up guests or to go across the lake to John Lewis's hotel," said Elizabeth A. Dear, an expert on Bull Head Lodge. Lewis was proud of his friendship with Russell and their yearly hunting trips. He not only introduced hotel guests to Russell, he also announced the couple as they entered the dining room, paid for their meals, and prominently displayed Russell's art in the lobby. And, he provided a cabin that Nancy used as an art sales room—where Charlie could stay after a night of drinking with guests.

"We often spent an evening with Charlie Russell, the cowboy artist, and his wife Nancy," recalled Cora Hutchings, an area resident. "He had a seemingly inexhaustible number [of stories] and a way of telling them so that even though we heard them over and over we still enjoyed them."

While tourists continued to arrive regularly at Lewis's on boats, Lewis early on recognized the automobile's potential. He realized that talk of a transmountain highway across Glacier, Going-to-the-Sun

Highway, was more than just idle speculation. It was inevitable—

the only question was how long until financing was approved. That would happen in 1921, with an initial $100,000 appropriation from Congress.

Rather than wait, Lewis spent over $3,000 in 1919 cutting three and a half miles of right of way along the lake, grading two miles of road and building three bridges. He was motivated by more than public goodwill; he knew traffic would pass his hotel, boosting business. Also, he and Harvey Apgar had subdivided lots northeast of the hotel in 1916 and were eager to sell the parcels, called Glacier Villa Sites, to summer visitors. Going-to-the-Sun road reached Lewis's hotel in 1922.

Accommodating automobile tourists required some renovations. The hotel had been designed for guests arriving via boat, and presented its best face to the lake. Cutter had not taken into account the possibility of people arriving at the rear, which served as an entrance for staff and riders. To increase the appeal of the east side of the building, Lewis added balconies and revised the lobby's lay-out.

The next year Lewis invited Cutter to plan a thirty-five- to forty-room addition. Cutter had pre-liminary plans ready in ten days. Upon reviewing them, Lewis wrote: "Mrs. Lewis has decided that she wants a 30-foot sun parlor leading from the old hotel to the new annex." After several days of thought, the Lewises decided against their own idea and telegraphed Cutter to stop the revisions. For reasons unknown, Lewis paid Cutter's $1,200 bill but never went ahead with the work. Instead, in 1927 Lewis added the Soda Fountain building and Garden Court.

Great Northern officials watched Going-to-the-Sun Highway's progress with appreciation mixed with apprehension. Like Lewis, they were strong backers of the road, expecting it to increase traffic to their hotels. Now, though, they began to fear a rival railway jumping in, either taking over Lewis's or setting up another hotel.

The Great Northern got a scare in 1927 when it learned that a team

On his regular trips to the Lewis (Glacier) Hotel, cowboy artist Charlie Russell sometimes visited the nearby Park Saddle Horse Company corrals, where he mixed readily with the wranglers. One of them, Ace Powell, became a Russell protege and went on to a career in painting, sketching and sculpting bronzes.

Lewis (Glacier) Hotel owner John Lewis was born in Iowa in 1865, and graduated in 1889 as a lawyer from Iowa State University, where he excelled at sports, particularly baseball. He played one season for a professional baseball team, being paid the unheard of salary of $2,500. He came to Montana's Flathead Valley in 1890, making his home in Columbia Falls and building its first hotel, The Columbia. He later took over the three-story Gaylord Hotel. He was a stalwart Republican and was appointed by President Theodore Roosevelt as the receiver of public money at the Kalispell Land Office.

from the Chicago, Milwaukee & St. Paul Railway was looking over Lake McDonald. "I think it's their intention to try to secure access to Glacier Park by auto from Missoula, similar to their experience via Gallatin Gateway to Yellowstone," vice-president William Kenney reported to Ralph Budd, president of the Great Northern. Budd immediately consulted Hill. "I do not feel that we should count on building a hotel at the head of Lake McDonald, near Lewis's," Hill replied. "We are not looking for chances to build hotels and I do not think tourists would stop there when the road is finished, but would go through to Sun Camp, St. Mary's etc."

In late 1928, despite Hill's stand, the Great Northern decided to try to buy Lewis's anyway. Rather than deal directly with John Lewis, given a history of barely civil relations, the Great Northern had Howard Hays act as an intermediary. Hays was relatively new to Glacier, but he had gotten to know the Lewises because his bus service, Glacier Park Transport Company, ran shuttles between the hotel and Belton Station.

The railway's initial offer was $200,000, more than three times the original cost. Lewis rejected it. Hays wrote a letter warning Lewis the federal government, which was trying to purchase private property in the park, might get the hotel by condemning it. Hays hinted it would be better to sell out now than later. Lewis held fast.

After letting the railway stew for a couple months, Lewis made a counteroffer, asking $350,000. Kenney thought Lewis "must be a little soft [in the head]," saying, "I think we can get this hotel much cheaper." Maybe, but Great Northern executives weren't going to take any chances and in February 1929 the executive committee resolved to pay between $300,000 and $325,000 for the hotel.

One of the reasons the railway was willing to boost what it would pay was discussions it was having with the Park Service. The service was anxious to reduce in-holdings, and Lewis's property was one of the largest pieces of private land to come on the block. The railway proposed buying the hotel, retaining ownership of the building, and selling the land to the government for $150,000.

As Lewis and the railway waited to see who would blink first, Lewis pulled a surprise, applying to build a hotel at Logan Pass. Budd was outraged. "Lewis is really playing with fire," he fumed, adding that Lewis must know if the Great Northern put up a hotel at McDonald Creek "he will have a meager chance to participate in any business."

Throughout the summer of 1929, the feud simmered. Lewis tried to get at the Great Northern by spreading rumors about service at Sperry Chalets, telling tourists they could not get lunch or accommodation

there so they had better take a meal with them and plan on camping or returning that day. In retaliation, A.J. Dickinson, Great Northern's passenger traffic agent, suggested the railway eliminate all references to Lewis in its publicity, cut all tours that included the hotel, and to try to keep people on the east side of the park.

It is not known whether word of this threat ever got to Lewis, but a month later, in February 1930, he agreed to the sale. It may or may not be coincidence that the stock market had collapsed a few months before, marking the start of the Great Depression, and Lewis, a savvy businessman then in his sixties, realized he was running out of time to make a good deal. Further pressure may have come from the passage of the Department of the Interior's Appropriations Act that empowered the Park Service to use condemnation proceedings to eliminate in-holdings. Lewis's Gaylord Hotel had burned in 1928, and some sources have speculated that and the 1929 fire at Half Moon, which burned for two weeks along the Lake McDonald shore, hastened the Lewises' willingness to sell.

The Great Northern purchased Lewis's hotel, its furnishings, and surrounding land through a subsidiary, the Dakota Development Company. In 1932, after discussions with the federal government, the railway sold the hotel and 285 acres to the National Park Service for half the $225,000 purchase price in return for a twenty-year lease on the facilities.

Captain William Swanson stands proudly at the prow of the newly finished DeSmet on its way to Lake McDonald in 1930. The excursion boat was named for the Jesuit priest who is said to have explored the Glacier area in 1845. Howard Hays, owner of the Glacier Park Transport Company, commissioned the boat. Swanson was a longtime boat builder in Glacier, having arrived in the park in 1914. Hays's company kept the DeSmet until 1953 when it was sold to Arthur M. Burch, whose family continues to operate it on the lake.

The two-story Snyder Hall, built in 1911, was where John Lewis held his dances and public assemblies. Cowboy artist Charlie Russell, who fancied himself as something of a "hoofer" after taking dancing lessons, regularly attended the shindigs with his wife Nancy. The hall has since been remodeled into a staff dormitory.

In an effort to cut ties to Lewis, Great Northern officials renamed the facility Lake McDonald Hotel. Other suggestions were to name it after Charlie Russell, who had died four years earlier, or George Bird Grinnell. Heaven's Peak Hotel was also considered. The presence of the Lewises was not entirely erased; they had a cabin near the hotel, and Olive remained as postmistress for Lake McDonald until 1944.

Before John Lewis died in 1934, he was able to see a long-held dream come true: completion of Going-to-the-Sun road in 1932 and its public opening in July 1933. It's estimated 40,000 cars went over Logan Pass that first summer—right by the hotel's back door. Soon, reconstruction of Going-to-the-Sun necessitated building the present loop road to access the lodge. A general store was opened in 1937, providing groceries and staples.

These additions, plus the boost to tourism caused by Going-to-the-Sun road, made Lake McDonald Hotel one of the park's most popular and busiest establishments, justifying the cost of its purchase for the railway and allowing the hotel to survive the Depression on a better footing than other Great Northern hotels and chalets.

"Clark Gable was a regular visitor," recalled Bill Wanser, who helped his parents operate Crossley Lake (now Cosley Lake) Tent Camp in the 1920s and 1930s. "The employees awaited his visits with great anticipation, and always expended spit and polish in preparing the hotel for his arrival. However, they always were disappointed. Gable's limousine and luggage would arrive at the lodge without him.

"The actor habitually alighted at the Lake McDonald corral to play stud poker with the cowboys," Wanser said. "The poker games went on till long after midnight. Gable, reputedly, always lost. The employees were disillusioned to learn that, after their long preparations, the great man had groped his way into the hotel at 3 o'clock in the morning, smelling of horse blankets, beer and cheap cigars."

In the hotel's basement, Great Northern staff found a collection of Indian artifacts. Too busy with the takeover, staff inventoried the items, then boxed and stored them. It would take almost two decades to sort out what to do with them.

At one point in the mid-1930s, James Ridler, who ran the gift shop concession, found the "Indian curios," and put some up for sale. Great Northern officials quickly retrieved the items and banned further sales. The staff of Chicago's Field Museum was consulted, and informed the railway of the collection's uniqueness: It contained items of clothing, drums, and tools from a variety of western tribes, including some that no longer existed. The value was pegged at $6,900, more than the price of an average house.

Periodically, the railway's comptroller reminded his bosses to do something with the collection. Little happened until the early 1950s when yet another Great Northern president, John Budd, was prodded about the unresolved situation. Budd turned over many items to the Museum of the Plains Indian in Browning, Montana where they joined donations from Louis Hill's personal collection. Other pieces went to the Field Museum and the Science Museum of Minnesota in St. Paul.

By the mid-1950s, time and the wear of thousands of tourists annually traipsing through Lake McDonald Hotel were taking their toll. Consumer expectations regarding comfort were rising; for instance, a washroom for each suite was expected. Upgrades and repairs were needed but the Great Northern and the National Park Service couldn't agree on details. It would be a familiar refrain over the next twenty years, as the railway, Donald Knutson and then Don Hummel each tried to negotiate improvements with the Park Service, with varying success.

The Great Northern ran into a roadblock because the Park Service wanted to abandon the hotel, tear it down, and build new facilities at Apgar. The idea was to create a tourist center at Apgar to service a paved road running north toward Kintla Lake and across the border into Alberta, creating a loop between Waterton and Glacier parks. (The road would never be paved or extended into Canada.) Despite repeated prodding to dump the site, Great Northern officials would not relent, and the hotel remained, but no significant upgrades were made. However, William R. Mackin did get to build the Apgar Village Inn

Steps made of quarter-cut logs and gnarled newel posts show a whimsical flair on the part of architect Kirtland Cutter, who designed Lake McDonald Lodge. Cutter was renowned for his Swiss-style and vernacular designs, although he was also responsible for the magnificent Davenport Hotel in Spokane. It was owner John Lewis who asked Cutter to keep the bark on the lobby columns. Extreme care had to be exercised in handling the columns to keep the bark intact, and Lewis himself supervised construction to ensure the job was done properly.

The rampaging flood waters of Snyder Creek washed away the foundation of the dining room fireplace in June 1964. The fireplace collapsed, taking with it part of the floor and leaving the rest of the room hanging. Staff had to work in a makeshift kitchen and dining room until repairs could be effected.

Chalet in 1956 at the foot of Lake Mcdonald, the first new visitor facility on the west side of the park in more than forty years.

When Knutson took over management of the hotel chain in 1957, he pressed for the addition of a motel, upgrades to the cottages (last modified in the 1940s with plumbing and bathrooms), and construction of a floating cocktail lounge on the lake. The lounge was nixed, but Knutson, with Great Northern financing, was able to get the Park Service to allow a wholesale revamp of the lobby, adding toilet facilities in ten rooms without baths, and modernizing the dining room and kitchen.

Much of the work in the dining room, kitchen, and lobby was undone by the 1964 flood. "Snyder Creek had rampaged down the mountain undermining huge cedar trees which formed a dam that diverted the flood directly into the hotel," Hummel recalled. "The dining room had been undermined, an empty shell hanging over eroded stream banks. Its floor lay at the bottom of the creek. The big stone fireplace that had stood at its far end was completely gone. Ragged logs and the tattered remains of its roof hung over empty space."

The dining room and kitchen were rebuilt, the lobby remodeled again, and the long-desired motel and coffee shop approved. Hummel, though, was stymied from further change by implementation in 1977 of Glacier Park's Final Master Plan which, among other things, put a cap on the number of guest rooms in the park. As a result, throughout the 1970s only minor changes were approved for Lake McDonald Lodge and its related facilities. Hummel sold Glacier Park Inc. in 1981.

For all the changes that have occurred to Lake McDonald Lodge over the years, the original Lewis building is mostly intact, and its significance remains unmarred. For the 660,000 people who annually drive Going-to-the-Sun Road, there is much here to be seen and appreciated. Visitors marvel at the drawings on the fireplace, according to myth done by Charlie Russell, and ogle the many hides and mounted heads hung by John Lewis. They can ride the *DeSmet* on the lake, imagining earlier eras when boats were the only way to reach the

hotel, or hike and ride to Sperry Glacier. Guests still sit on the lakeside "front" porch to watch the sun set behind the mountains, as tourists have done for generations.

In 1976, the cultural significance of the lodge was recognized when it was added to the National Register of Historic Places; in 1987, it also was declared a National Historic Landmark.

The patchwork of repairs, renovations, and upgrades the building has incurred over the past five decades have held the structures together, but just barely. "Much remains to be done," according to a 1990s National Park Service report. Estimates from the park service indicated it would cost between $23 million and $47 million to bring the lodge and related facilities to modern standards and ensure they remain open to tourists for decades to come.

The view from the lakeside at Lake McDonald Lodge has had the same effect on tourists for ages. The tranquillity almost demands guests sit and take in the scene "for a spell."

2843 Belton Chalets

Belton Chalets were the first facilities built and opened by the Great Northern to serve Glacier National Park. The Swiss chalet styling, a variation of what is called "parkitecture," was not always recognized in the early days. The first manager of the hotel wrote Great Northern headquarters to suggest that a sign was needed "indicating it is a stopping place for the public as a great many of the traveling public do not comprehend the meaning of the word chalet."

— *Chapter 12* —
Belton Chalets

Belton Chalets and the rest of the hotels built by the Great Northern for Glacier Park owe their existence to engineer John F. Stevens, who later served two years as chief engineer on the Panama Canal project. Although Stevens had nothing directly to do with the construction of the chalets, his locating Marias Pass in 1889 led to a series of events culminating in the creation of Glacier Park and commission of the facilities. Belton Chalets, unfortunately, would never pull their weight for the railway in developing park tourism.

In Stevens' time the Glacier region was relatively unexplored, except by natives and miners, and uninhabited. Constructing the Great Northern's transcontinental line through Marias Pass in 1891 brought settlers, Belton being one of the first towns to spring up. By one story, Belton got its name from Daniels Webster Bell, who took up a claim near the site. The Civil War veteran served as a camp cook for railway location parties during construction through the pass.

It was a relatively tranquil existence for Bell and fellow settlers Milo Apgar, Charles Howe, and Ed Dow until the Great Northern began passenger service in June 1893. Its trains took thousands of people a year through Marias Pass and, as word of the region's scenic beauty spread, people became curious about Glacier country. Dow, Apgar, Howe, and George Snyder soon recognized the tourism potential of Lake McDonald. Dow constructed a hotel at Belton, Apgar cabins at the site of today's Village Inn, and Snyder a hotel near the head of the lake.

Great Northern officials watched the increasing use of Belton as a stop-off. By 1909 it seemed likely that a third push to have Glacier

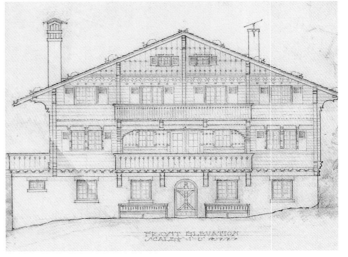

Architectural rendition of Belton Chalets' main building. While the sketch resembles the main chalet, the first structure built (1910), it is not known what company was awarded the design job.

Belton Chalets, Western Gateway to
Glacier National Park, Montana.

Belton Chalets were expanded for the second and last time in 1913 with the construction of a twenty-four-bedroom annex, or dorm as it was called. Guests using the 104-by-35-foot, three-story annex had to share communal bathrooms on the two sleeping levels. The basement held storage rooms and a hall for gatherings. Curiously, although the dorm was wired for electricity and there was a generator on site that provided power for the main chalet, the bedroom annex also had hardware for gas lamps and was initially fueled by an acetylene plant.

become a national park would succeed, and the railway wanted in on the ground floor. In April, it approved money to build a depot and hotel at Belton.

Across from Belton Station, at the base of a moss-covered cliff in a grove of larch and birch trees, the first building of what would become Belton Chalets was started: a three-story, ten-room hotel with dining room and kitchen. "Camp 10," as it was sometimes later referred to by railway officials who numbered each of their sites, was built on a five-acre plot leased until 1919 from the U.S. Forest Service. It is not known who designed the building. Although the architectural firm of Cutter and Malmgren of Spokane submitted preliminary drawings, there is no evidence it got the job, and the result bears only passing resemblance to its submission. Also lost to history is the name of the contractor who built the chalet, the first commissioned by the Great Northern to take advantage of tourism to Glacier.

Belton Chalet opened for business June 27, 1910. The Great Northern assured area residents that it was not an establishment exclusive to the wealthy. "The impression has gotten abroad that the rates will be $4 or over, but this is a mistake; $2 entitles everyone to all there is in the big show including the side shows," a railway official wrote the editor of the *Whitefish Pilot*.

As Belton Chalet was the Great Northern's first Glacier facility, there was no precedent for its operation. The formation of Glacier

Park Hotel Company was four years off, so responsibility fell to the superintendent of dining and sleeping cars, although Louis Hill was directly, and quite actively, involved.

Great Northern headquarters' staff were sticklers for detail. When, at the end of the 1910 season, the accounting department discovered the balance sheet was out five cents, the auditor wrote: "Will you kindly instruct the agent at this hotel to remit the amount short." The auditor had cause for concern; Belton Chalets ran at a loss that first summer. After puzzling over various options to increase business, the railway decided to cut its room rate by fifty cents a night.

The idea of running the chalet for only the three-month summer tourist season was anathema to railroad officials, who were used to year-round operations. During the winter of 1910-1911, the Great Northern leased the premises to Glacier superintendent William Logan for the use of park rangers while permanent accommodations for park staff were being built at Fish Creek.

Belton Chalets opened in 1911 with Fiammetta Fery as manager. Her father was artist John Fery, on contract with the Great Northern to paint landscapes of the park. Fery's deal with the railway included jobs for his daughters at Glacier's chalets. Also that summer the railway added three more buildings at Belton: two cabins, and a third structure known as "The Studio." With a huge skylight, the five-bedroom, 32-by-53-foot Studio was meant for the use of artists; it is not known if Fery ever occupied it.

A special seven-car Great Northern train carrying residents of Columbia Falls and Kalispell stops at Belton on Sunday, June 22, 1913, to pick up passengers. They were headed for Midvale to spend the day touring the newly opened Glacier Park Hotel and grounds. Upon their arrival, the railway served them a free dinner. The group was accompanied by the Kalispell Elks Club band, resplendent in their white uniforms. James Shoemaker, who organized the event, was so taken with the Elks he told newspaper reporters he wanted to make the group the official Glacier Park band.

The Spokane architectural firm of Cutter and Malmgren submitted this illustration as part of a package of preliminary drawings in the hope of winning the contract to design Belton Chalets.

Louis Hill wasn't above taking a direct role in boosting use of Belton Chalets. He encouraged those participating in the Twin Cities–to–Helena auto tour in July to extend their trip to Glacier. Hill led the way in a car he had shipped from St. Paul, Minnesota taking an unfinished and previously untested route between Kalispell and Belton, Montana.

"Everybody get out and give the glad hand to president Hill and his party of autos," the Kalispell *Daily Inter Lake* urged its readers. Kalispell residents waited until the road was completed in September 1911 to make the trip. "The old 'tote' road, frequently crossing the new highway, speaks silently of conditions that are gone forever," the *Inter Lake* noted.

Unfortunately, the Kalispell tour was too late in the season to help Belton Chalets, which ended the summer $1,500 in the hole. Expenses were $3,431.11 with earnings tallying just $1,929.41.

A Concord coach, or tally-ho, pulled by teams of two or four horses, provided the only means of getting from Belton (now West Glacier) to Apgar before the start of bus service. Belton hotelier Ed Dow set up the earliest tally-ho. The coach could carry eight to ten passengers, who shared the rental fee of $27.50 (as of 1915). Trips were not to exceed thirty miles a day. Later, tally-hos were used at Glacier Park Hotel and Many Glacier Hotel as a novelty shuttle service.

When business at the chalets proved no better for a third summer, 1912, Hill intervened. In late July he struck a deal to let Bill Brewster occupy and operate the chalets rent-free. No known records indicate how Brewster did, but he apparently lasted just one season.

Brewster did show some ingenuity in trying to build business. Long after he'd vacated the premises, a railway auditor turned up a charge of $15.29 for feeding bear cubs. "Will you please advise if this is an expense that should be taken care of [by us]?" auditor F.E. Draper asked Howard Noble, general manager of the Great Northern. Charge it to the Glacier Park operations, Noble advised, in an apparent attempt to sweep the matter under the carpet.

For the 1913 season, a fifth building, a twenty-four-bedroom annex, was added along with enlargement of the dining room and kitchen, bringing to $60,000 the railway's investment at Belton. Construction of the annex was handled by a crew of twenty workmen for E.G. Evensta, the contractor Great Northern had also hired to build Glacier

Park Hotel. With completion of the "guest dormitory," Belton Chalets had a capacity for 118 people. The dining room capacity went from sixteen to fifty people.

The Belton expansion was timed for the official opening of Glacier Park Hotel and the rest of the railway's chalet system for the 1913 season. Hill was anxious not to have his facilities overwhelmed by the flood of tourists expected for 1913. And come tourists did.

Hill's best intentions aside, Belton Chalets would never prove themselves a tourist attraction or a benefit to the bottom line of the hotel company. For the next thirty years, the chalet complex offered decent meals and accommodations, but never fulfilled the role of the railway's western gatekeeper to Glacier Park.

Their profitability was undermined primarily by location. Belton Chalets are not in the park, which is where visitors wanted to be. John Muir, the father of the American conservation movement, noted the situation accurately. "Get off the track at Belton Station, and in a few minutes you will find yourself in the midst of what you are sure to say is the best care-killing scenery on the continent," Muir said. Passengers arriving at Belton faced a choice of paying for a room for the night at the chalets or fifty cents for the stage to Lake McDonald, where they could tent, hike, or take trail and boat rides. Almost invariably they chose the latter. The hour-long ride through hemlock and red cedars to the lake was refreshing after the train ride. Staff at Belton Chalets had little chance to direct visitors to Great Northern's facilities on the park's east side.

It also didn't help that, in all the years Great Northern owned Belton

These tickets stubs for a trip from Seattle to Chicago include a two-night stopover in Glacier. The passenger took the trip across Going-to-the-Sun road "backwards," going from Belton to East Glacier. More typical was the other direction. Great Northern encouraged stopovers, even as short as one day, expecting that a brief glimpse at Glacier's magnificent scenery would almost certainly lure visitors back for a longer stay.

Chalets, tours never started or ended there.

Like the rest of the railway's hotels, Belton Chalets suffered a drastic loss of business during World War I. In February 1917, Congress gave Glacier Park Hotel Company the right to purchase the land on which the Belton Chalets were built. In 1919, the Great Northern exercised its option, and shelled out $1,272.50 for the parcel.

The disillusionment Great Northern officials felt over continued red ink at Belton Chalets showed in 1923 when they indicated they might be willing to sell. George W. Slack, president of Belton Mercantile Company, looking for a bargain, offered the railway $10,000. In a change of heart, Hill refused Slack's bid, stating "business at the Belton Chalets will be good for a longer season" when the road to Logan Pass summit is completed in "two or three years." It was a costly decision. The road from Belton to the summit, the western leg of Going-to-the-Sun Highway, was not completed until 1929.

During the glory days of train travel to Glacier, Belton Chalets were closed for four summers, 1926 to 1929, due to lack of business. When they reopened in 1930, only rooms were rented; no meals were served.

When Going-to-the-Sun road finally opened in 1933, Belton

The Empire Builder was Great Northern's premier train and was outfitted accordingly. The lounge car, left, offered passengers a comfortable place to relax, read, write letters, or play cards. The railway provided stationery, and playing cards could be purchased for whist, rummy, and bridge. At night, the resident of the bottom bunk in the Empire Builder's Pullman cars could turn off the light, open the blind and watch the lights of the countryside pass by or just gaze at the stars.

Belton Chalets were renowned for their beautiful landscaping, until the construction of Highway 2 forced the removal of the gardens and trellis-covered walkway to the train depot. A yardman who also served as baggage handler for train passengers, greeter and bellman at the chalet tended the grounds. Such was the beauty of this horticultural oasis that it led to a man stepping off the train to declare: "Is this Glacier Park? Why, it's not as big as Manitou city park in Spokane."

Chalets benefited only marginally. Railway officials should have known there'd be little value for the chalets from what had happened in 1930 with the completion of Highway 2 between Belton and Midvale (now East Glacier Park). Highway 2 passed between the station and Belton Chalets, forcing removal of a vine-covered connecting path, but proximity to motorists made little difference to business.

Hoping to capitalize on day traffic, the hotel company in 1934 adopted the European plan, where guests were charged separately for bed and board. Under the previous American plan, a patron was charged $4.50 for meals and a room with a single bed. Without meals included, rooms rented for $1.50 for a single bed and $2.25 for a double, making prices more competitive with those charged by local cabin camps.

Belton Chalets struggled on through the Depression, when it was open only periodically. Its guest count declined as time went on, from 118 to 72 people, thus reducing overhead. Like the rest of Great Northern's hotel chain, it was closed from 1943 to 1945 during World War II. Glacier Park Hotel Company did not bother reopening Belton Chalets after the war, and they were sold in June 1946 to William A. Murrell for $25,550. It was the beginning of a series of ownership changes.

On August 1, 1949, the chalets were sold to H.A. Berryman for $35,000. This was just as construction was starting on nearby Hungry Horse Dam, and accommodations for workers were in short supply.

It may have been an opportune time to be in the hotel business, but Berryman did not stick it out. In June 1951 he sold the chalets to Albert and Mildred A. Gunn of Spokane for $55,000.

Later in the 1950s, the chalets were sold to Grant and Virginia Spears, who tried to make the facility an art colony. Like other attempts, it did not last. The Belton Chalets would change hands again, ending up in the 1960s as a pizzeria.

Repeated sale of the property slowed when Ross and Kathleen (Kay) Luding purchased the chalets in 1970. Lanny Luding said his parents bought Belton Chalets—minus The Studio, which had been sold by a previous owner— to fulfill a requirement by the National Park Service that they have a reservation system for Granite Park and Sperry Chalets, which they also managed. Belton Chalets Inc. was established in 1971, based here, to take reservations and act as supply depot for the other chalets.

Three-year-old Karola Miener plays checkers with Isabel Dawson on the deck of Belton Chalets. Dawson was the wife of Midvale pioneer resident Tom Dawson and sister of another Midvale pioneer, Horace Clarke. Isabel's son, John Clarke, was a sculptor renowned for the fact he was deaf and mute. Karola's parents, Charles and Berta Mankenberg, worked in and around Glacier more than two decades. Charles was a teacher. Berta had been a leading mezzo-soprano in Germany prior to emigrating to America, but could find no work in her new homeland due to anti-German sentiment caused by the outbreak of World War I.

The Luding family tried to make Belton Chalets pay for themselves in the 1970s by occasionally renting rooms and running a bar and restaurant from the main chalet. Family matriarch Kay Luding toyed with the idea of restoring the structures, but was never able to undertake the project. When the Luding family business was jolted by the 1992 closure of Sperry and Granite Park chalets because of environmental problems, they decided to sell Belton Chalets.

The 3.5-acre tract was bought in June 1997 by the team of Andy Baxter and Cas Still of Polson, Montana. "We had been looking for a big project for several years," said Still, who had been in the restoration business in Florida with her husband before moving to Montana.

The balconies of the sleeping annex at Belton Chalets were falling apart when the complex was bought by Andy Baxter and Cas Still in 1997. The buildings have since been meticulously restored.

Over the next two years, Baxter and Still invested more than $1 million to have general contractors Kingston Construction of Bigfork, Montana, and Leo Keane North Country Builders of Whitefish, Montana, renovate and restore Belton Chalets. A Florida architect aided them. "Our plan was to clean it up, do the basic restoration and turn it over," Still said. "But once we got into it, we couldn't stop.... We found so much, like original furniture, that we kept on going."

The work included all new wiring, new plumbing, rebuilding balconies and, in the bedroom annex, creating a private bath in each room. "We had to work out some delicate plans to put bathrooms in the rooms and still stay true to the historic nature of the building," Still said. The tiptoeing around design issues was necessary because all four Belton Chalet buildings were listed on the National Register of Historic Places. (They have since been added to the list of National Historic Landmarks.) Work on the main building and cabins was completed in 1998, and they opened for business on the Memorial Day weekend. The bedroom annex was finished in 1999.

For travelers looking for a historic getaway, Belton Chalets are a nostalgic treat, offering a glimpse at the early days of tourism to Glacier. They are open seven months a year, from Memorial Day to mid-October.

The lobby of the bedroom annex at Belton Chalets is resplendent following a two-year restoration that opened the chalets to the public for the first time in nearly three decades.

The two three-bedroom cabins, twenty-six by twenty-seven feet, were built in 1911 to expand the sleeping capacity of the original Belton Chalets. They featured inside bathrooms with running water, electric lighting and stoves for heat. Following their restoration in 1999, they were named for explorers Lewis and Clark.

163

For Further Reading

A Selected Bibliography

RAY DJUFF COLLECTION

This brochure for the Prince of Wales Hotel was printed to help revive business after the hotel had been closed for three summers during the Depression. It is one of the few times any hotel in the Great Northern's chain was singled out for promotion separate from the rest.

Buchholtz, C.W. *Man in Glacier*. 2nd edition. West Glacier, Mont.: Glacier Natural History Association, 1993.

Christopherson, Edmund. *Adventure Among the Glaciers*. Missoula, Mont.: Earthquake Press, 1966.

Creese, Walter L. *The Crowning of the American Landscape: Eight Great Spaces and Their Buildings*. Princeton, N.J.: Princeton University Press, 1985.

Deittert, Gerald A. *Grinnell's Glacier: George Bird Grinnell and Glacier National Park*. Missoula, Mont.: Mountain Press Publishing Company, 1992.

Diehl-Taylor, Christiane. "Passengers, Profits and Prestige: The Glacier Park Hotel Company, 1914-1929." *Montana: The Magazine of Western History*. Summer 1997.

Dillon, Tom. *Over the Trails of Glacier National Park*. St. Paul, Minn: Great Northern Railway, circa 1911.

Getty, Ian. *The History of Human Settlement in Waterton Lakes National Park 1800-1937. A research paper prepared for the Historic Parks Branch*. Calgary, Alta.: Parks Canada, 1971.

Great Northern Railway company records. The bulk of records related to the railway are held at the Minnesota Historical Society archives in St. Paul, Minn. For this work, the authors consulted the files on the Glacier Park Company and records in the president's subject files related to Glacier and Waterton Lakes national parks.

Hagen, John. *A History of Many Glacier Hotel*. Minneapolis, Minn.: Glacier Park Foundation Inc., 1985.

Hanna, Warren L. *Montana's Many-Splendored Glacierland*. Seattle, Wash.: Superior Publishing Company, 1976.

Hart, Edward John. *The Brewster Story: From Pack Train to Tour Bus*. Banff, Alta.: Brewster Transport Company Ltd., 1981.

Hays, Howard H., Sr., and H.A. Noble. *Drivers' Manual*. 8th edition. East Glacier, Mont.: Glacier Park Transport Company, 1949.

Hidy, Ralph W., Muriel E. Hidy, and Roy V. Scott, with Don L. Hofsommer. *The Great Northern Railway: A History*. Boston, Mass.: Harvard Business School Press, 1988.

Hill, Louis Warren, Sr. The business and personal papers of Louis Hill are in archives at James Jerome Hill Reference Library in St. Paul, Minn.

Hummel, Don. *Wake Up, America! The Environmentalists are Stealing the National Parks: The Destruction of Concessions and Public Access*. Bellevue, Wash.: The Free Enterprise Press, 1987.

Lambert, Kirby. "The Lure of the Parks." *Montana: The Magazine of Western History*. Spring 1996.

Malone, Michael. *James J. Hill: Empire Builder of the Northwest*. Oklahoma City, Okla.: University of Oklahoma Press, 1996.

Martin, Albro. *James J. Hill and the Opening of the Northwest*. New York: Oxford University Press, 1976.

Matthews, Henry. "The Search for a Northwest Vernacular: Kirtland Cutter and the Rustic Picturesque 1888-1920," in *Art and the National Dream: The Search for Vernacular Expression in Turn-of-the-Century Design.* Edited by Nicola Gordon Bowe. Dublin, Ireland: Irish Academic Press, 1993.

Matthews, Henry C. *Kirtland Cutter: Architect in the Land of Promise.* Seattle, Wash.: University of Washington Press, 1998.

National Park Service archives, West Glacier, Mont. Superintendents' reports, park brochures, correspondence between the park service and concessioners, and files related to specific topics about the park.

Newell, Alan, et. al. *Historic Resources Study, Glacier National Park and Historic Structures Survey.* Denver, Colo.: Glacier National Park, 1980.

Newspapers: *Calgary Herald,* (Kalispell, MT) *Daily Inter-Lake,* (Columbia Falls, MT) *Hungry Horse News, Great Falls* [Montana] *Tribune,* (Columbia Falls, MT) *Columbian, Kalispell* [Montana] *Times, The Lethbridge* [Alberta] *Herald,* (Missoula, MT) *Missoulian, New York Times, St. Paul Dispatch, St. Paul Pioneer Press, Whitefish* [Montana] *Pilot.*

Ober, Michael J. "Enmity and Alliance: Park Service-Concessioner Relations in Glacier National Park, 1892-1961." Unpublished MA thesis, University of Montana, 1973.

Pomeroy, Earl. *In Search of the Golden West: The Tourist in Western America.* New York: Alfred A. Knopf, 1957.

Reiss, Winold, and F.B. Linderman. *Blackfeet Indians.* St. Paul, Minn.: Great Northern Railway, 1935.

Robinson, Donald H. *Through the Years in Glacier National Park.* West Glacier, Mont.: Glacier Natural History Association, 1960.

Ruhle, George. *Guide to Glacier National Park.* Minneapolis, Minn.: Campbell-Mithun, Inc., 1949.

Runte, Alfred. "Promoting Wonderland: Western Railroads and the Evolution of National Park Advertising." *Journal of the West.* January 1992.

Schultz, James Willard. *Recently Discovered Tales of Life Among the Indians.* Compiled and edited by Warren L. Hanna. Missoula, Mont.: Mountain Press Publishing Company, 1988.

Shankland, Robert. *Steve Mather of the National Parks.* New York: Alfred A. Knopf, 1970.

Tanner, Scott J. "A Biography of Winold Reiss: The Man Who Created the Great Northern Railway's Blackfeet Indian Portraits." Great Northern Railway Historical Society reference sheet No. 242. June 1996.

Toltz King Duvall Anderson and Associates, St. Paul, Minn. Architectural drawings and sketches and photographs made by employees in 1926-27 for Great Northern Railway for a hotel in Waterton Lakes National Park, Alta.

Thompson, Margaret. *High Trails of Glacier National Park.* Caldwell, Idaho: The Caxton Printers, Ltd., 1936.

Wood, C.R. *Lines West: A Pictorial History of Great Northern Railway Operations 1887-1967.* Seattle, Wash.: Superior Publishing Company, 1967.

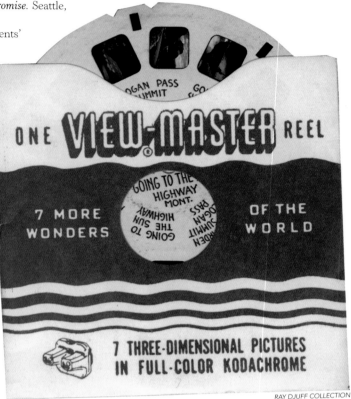

RAY DJUFF COLLECTION

The View-Master was first introduced at the New York World's Fair in 1939. This multi-reel series of Glacier was produced in the mid-1940s. One reel shows part of the main hall at Going-to-the-Sun Chalets, which looks distinctly dilapidated. It was one of the last pictures taken of the chalet site, which would soon be torn down. Renowned Glacier photographer Tomer Hileman never worked for View-Master, but did take images for its rival Tru-Vue, some of the few Hileman took in color.

Great Northern often worked in concert with Montana dude ranches to promote summer vacations.
RAY DJUFF COLLECTION

Index